Strategic Writing for UX

Drive Engagement, Conversion, and Retention with Every Word

Torrey Podmajersky

Beijing · Boston · Farnham · Sebastopol · Tokyo

Strategic Writing for UX
by Torrey Podmajersky

Published by O'Reilly Media, Inc., 1005 Gravenstein Highway North, Sebastopol, CA 95472.

O'Reilly books may be purchased for educational, business, or sales promotional use. Online editions are also available for most titles (*http://oreilly.com*). For more information, contact our corporate/institutional sales department: (800) 998-9938 or *corporate@oreilly.com*.

Acquisitions Editor: Jess Haberman
Developmental Editor: Angela Rufino
Production Editor: Kristen Brown
Copyeditor: Octal Publishing Services, Inc.
Proofreader: Rachel Monaghan
Indexer: Lucie Haskins

Cover Designer: Karen Montgomery
Interior Designers: Ron Bilodeau and Monica Kamsvaag
Illustrator: Rebecca Demarest
Compositor: Kristen Brown

June 2019: First Edition.

Revision History for the First Edition:

2020-06-19	Fifth release
2020-09-18	Sixth release

See *http://oreilly.com/catalog/errata.csp?isbn=0636920235583* for release details.

978-1-492-04939-5

[LSI]

[*contents*]

[*Preface*]

UX WRITING IS THE process of creating the words in user experiences (UX): the titles, buttons, labels, instructions, descriptions, notifications, warnings, and controls that people see. It's also the setup information, first-run experience, and how-to content that gives people confidence to take the next step.

When an organization depends on individual humans performing specific behaviors like buying tickets for events, playing a game, or riding public transit, words are ubiquitous and effective. Words can be seen on screens, signs, posters, and articles, as well as heard from devices and videos. The text can be minimal, but is very valuable.

But what do those words do, how do we choose them, and how do we know when they work? This book provides strategies to use UX writing to help meet people's goals while advancing our organizations toward converting, engaging, supporting, and reattracting those people. We structure our voice throughout the content so that the brand is recognizable to its audience. We apply common UX text patterns to ease and democratize the task of writing, and we measure how effective the UX content is.

Who Should Read This Book

If you need to write UX content on top of your usual job, you might be a marketing professional, technical writer, UX designer, product owner, or a software engineer. This book equips you with knowledge about what goals the UX content can accomplish, frameworks for writing it, and methods to measure it.

If you are or will be a UX writer, or if you're a manager or leader who wants to support a UX writer on your team, this book also gives you methods to demonstrate the value of UX writing and the impact it makes. In this book, you'll find processes and tools to do the work of writing and the work of partnering with design, business, legal, engineering, product, and other stakeholders sanely, creatively, and scalably.

How This Book Is Organized

Chapter 1 explains why UX content matters and how it integrates with the software development life cycle.

Chapter 2 provides a framework for the voice of the experience to align the UX content with the product principles.

Chapter 3 describes a process of content-first design for UX text, rooted in conversation.

Chapter 4 provides 11 patterns for UX text and demonstrates how they work in the three different voices of the example experiences.

Chapter 5 presents a four-phase process of editing UX text to be purposeful, concise, conversational, and clear.

Chapter 6 outlines three methods to measure the effect and quality of UX content: direct measurement, UX research, and heuristic analysis.

Chapter 7 recommends tools and processes for UX writing, including drafting text, managing content review, and tracking the work.

Chapter 8 shares my 30-60-90-day plan to ramp up and be successful as the first UX content professional in a team.

Chapter 9 concludes with advice about prioritizing UX writing work to be done.

Examples throughout this book come from three fictional organizations and experiences:

- The Sturgeon Club app, for members of a social club

- 'appee, a social game in which players compete by uploading images

- TAPP, an app for people who use a regional transit system

For clarity, I've narrowed down the terms for the most important ideas in this book:

- *Experience* is the app, software, or other designed interaction the organization is creating for which the UX writer is creating UX content.

- *Organization* is the civic body, public institution, private company, or other entity that makes or commissions the experience.

- *Team* is the group of humans a UX writer collaborates with.

- *People* are the humans who use the experiences. Specific terms for people depend on the experience: people who use The Sturgeon Club are *members*, people who use 'appee are *players*, and people who use TAPP are *riders*.

- *UX writer* is the generic title I use for the team member who has the responsibility for the UX content. Other titles used in the industry include *UX content strategist, content designer, content developer*, and *copywriter*.

- *UX content* is the output of the UX writer's work that directly helps people to use the experience. *UX text* is the subset of UX content that are the words used by interfaces. Other industry names for UX text include *microcopy, editorial, UI text*, and *strings*.

Why I Wrote This Book

UX content has been my professional focus for the past nine years. I started as a UX writer in Xbox in 2010, creating experiences for the millions of people playing on the Xbox 360 console, Xbox Live, and Xbox One. Then, I worked on the Microsoft account, and was the first UX writer for Microsoft Family and Microsoft Education. I was the first UX writer and content strategist for the OfferUp.com marketplace, which helps millions of Americans buy and sell in their communities. As I finish this book, I am the first UX content strategist for two teams at Google.

I love making experiences that help people. For me, that includes making experiences that help people become UX writers. I want more colleagues, more UX writers who are developing even better methods to create great experiences. We UX writers haven't had a common set of frameworks, tools, or methods that address the unique challenges of UX content. The organizations and managers who want to hire us might know they have a "word problem," but they have a hard time figuring out who to hire, how to support us, and what impact to expect.

This book was conceived when I realized that we can't have a community or discipline of UX writing until we hold some basic ideas in common. We need to share expectations for what UX content can do, best practices for making the content do what it can, and methods to measure its effect. I wrote this book to share my frameworks, tools, and methods for creating UX content, and to share my encouragement and enthusiasm for using UX content to help people and organizations meet their goals.

Acknowledgments

Thank you to my teams at Xbox, Windows, Microsoft Education, OfferUp, and Google. Everything I know about UX writing, I learned while working with you wonderful people. Thanks especially to those who pushed me to create better text, to find better solutions, to delight our customers and exceed the expectations of the business. I love working on challenging problems with you.

Thank you, Michelle Larez Mooney, for teaching me how to write UX. You were on my first interview loop to become a UX writer, and you taught me the craft. You showed me by example how to partner effectively with engineering, product, and localization teams. Even more, you demonstrated how to engage so deeply and so effectively that the value of the work was undeniable.

Thank you, Elly Searle, for having the idea and drive to make the first UX Writing course. You talked me into it and then went out and made it real by talking to Larry Asher at the School of Visual Concepts. I've learned so much from you about articulating what I can offer and asking for what I need. It has been a joy to teach with you and to benefit from your insights, enthusiasm, and dedication.

Thank you, Michaela Hutfles, for your coaching, mentorship, and friendship. My career in UX would be neither possible nor joyful without your reflection, advice, and encouragement.

Thank you, Nathan Crowder, Jeremy Zimmerman, Dawn Vogel, Sarah Grant, and the rest of our Type 'n' Gripe. I am a writer because we have written together every week for more than 12 years. Together we started pitching our fiction stories to top markets, instead of "easy" markets, regardless of rejection. I wouldn't have pitched this book without that practice, nor had the discipline to see it through.

Thank you, Jess Haberman and Angela Rufino and the rest of the astonishing team at O'Reilly, for believing in this book, suggesting paths forward, and supporting the entire process. Thank you also to my early readers and technical reviewers who helped to make this book more readable and more helpful.

And finally, thank you, Dietrich Podmajersky, my amazing partner. Your confidence that what I do matters more than housework, your support while I overcommit my time and energy, your patience for my inability to figure out when it's time to go to bed, and more all add up to make the thousands of ways you made this book possible. I love you.

[1]

Why: Meet the Goals of People and the Organization

If you think good design is expensive, you should look at the cost of bad design.

—RALF SPETH, CEO OF JAGUAR LAND ROVER

"WE NEED TO HIRE someone to fix the words!" I have heard this phrase from multiple people on teams I've worked on and UX leaders I've talked with. In each case, the person can point to the places in the experience where the words are "broken." These people have recognized that fixing the words would help their organization or the people who use their experiences advance in some important way.

In each case I've seen, there is enough "fixing" to keep a person busy for years, but fixing the words will never be enough. Consider this metaphor: an experience with broken words is a house with broken walls. Fix the words as you would repair the walls.

If there's only one broken wall, and it was built robustly, and the hole doesn't affect the electrical, plumbing, or architectural support the building needs, we can fix it cheaply. When an experience is built with consistent terminology, voice, information architecture, and ways to find, maintain, internationalize, and update its content, all we would need to do is fix the words.

When those things haven't been considered, and the breaks go through electrical, plumbing, or supporting timbers, then words can't fix the hole by themselves.

We will need a strategic approach to fix the underlying experience. We'll need to apply some engineering—in this case, UX writing—to fix the walls and support the building.

As an added benefit: fixing those walls will make the whole building stronger.

The strategic purpose of UX content is to meet two sets of goals: the goals of the organization responsible for the experience, and the goals of the people using the experience.

Align the Goals of the People and the Organization

Let's consider the goals of our first fictional example organization: the TAPP Transit System. The TAPP Transit System is a regional transit system in a city. TAPP, like any transit system, is under constant pressure to reduce costs and demonstrate its effectiveness. It also needs to bring in money through fares and taxes to maintain the vehicle fleet and pay its personnel.

TAPP cares about getting people to ride a bus for the first time, but that's not enough. TAPP needs to build a relationship with its population so that they choose to ride again and choose to support the transit system through their political choices. The transit system needs to establish a *virtuous cycle* of engaging and reengaging its riders.

The cycle starts when the organization attracts people to it (Figure 1-1). Then, it needs to convert those people. But because this is an experience and not just a sale, we need to onboard people into the experience, to set them up for success in it. Then, people can be engaged in the experience.

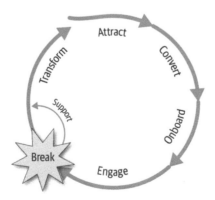

FIGURE 1-1

The organization's view of the experience virtuous cycle. Starting at the top, the organization attracts people to the experience, converts them, onboards them, and then engages them into the experience. To complete the virtuous cycle, we must transform engaged people into fans who attract others to the experience and who are reattracted themselves.

The virtuous part of the cycle comes next. The organization reaps tremendous benefit if it can transform people using the experience into fans. When someone is a fan of the experience, they not only prefer to use it themselves, but they recommend it to other people, helping the organization attract new people. This transformation can happen because the experience is excellent, it's useful to them, and, like any good brand, it reflects back to the person what they want to believe about themselves.

The transformation can even happen when the experience breaks. Whatever the cause of the break (natural disaster, bad bus driver, etc.), the organization can either lose the person or support them. By supporting the people in the experience, it can retain and engage those people further. When an organization plans for potential breaks and fixes them ahead of time, it not only can continue to engage the person, it can use the break as a moment to transform a person who is merely engaged into a fan.

The local people TAPP wants to attract just want to get to work, to school, to the doctor, to the grocery store. Riding the bus might be their best option, but they need to be aware of it and trust it. They are likely unaware of the transit system's organizational goals. They probably aren't considering the variety of needs other riders might have, nor the larger goals the transit system might have. They're probably worried about all the ways their ride could go wrong: incorrect fare, missing a transfer, full bus, and more.

We need to understand the cycle from the point of view of the people who will use the experience, to meet them where they are (Figure 1-2). Their first task is to investigate and verify what they know about the system. They aren't expecting to be attracted into the system, and they aren't thinking about becoming part of the transit system's virtuous cycle. They just want to know their options.

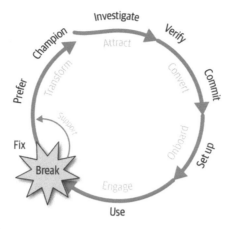

FIGURE 1-2

In the virtuous cycle, the organization and the person using the experience have different perspectives. While the organization attracts, converts, onboards, engages, supports, and transforms, the person investigates, verifies, commits to, sets up, uses, fixes, prefers, and champions the experience. By realizing this difference in perspective and focus, the organization can more effectively address what the person is there for.

Where TAPP is trying to attract the person, the person is investigating and verifying that they'll get where they want to go, on time. Where TAPP is concerned with converting, the person is deciding or committing to the experience. Where TAPP wants to onboard and engage the person, the person expects to get on the bus, pay, ride, and arrive at their destination.

The frequent TAPP rider tends to influence their communities to ride the bus. Through their behavior, they make riding the bus seem easy. Whether they think of themselves as champions of public transit or not, these people help attract more riders into the TAPP transit system.

Choose Content to Meet the Goals

Throughout the virtuous cycle, content helps the organization and the people using the experience meet their goals. What kind of content will help varies according to where the people are in the cycle.

At the beginning of the cycle, marketing content helps TAPP attract people to become riders. People interact with this content to investigate and verify that the experience will be right for them. This content is the traditional marketing of advertisements and press releases; the social media content of tweets, blogs, and posts; and more. It is the articles written in journals, the reviews and product ratings that are promoted on websites, and the product pages in app stores (Figure 1-3).

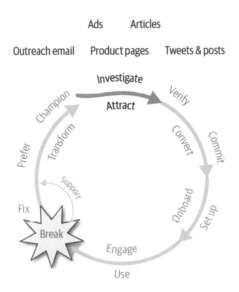

Ads   Articles

Outreach email   Product pages   Tweets & posts

FIGURE 1-3
For a person investigating whether an experience will work for them, traditional marketing content is appropriate, including ads, product pages, and more. These pieces of content meet the organizational goal of attracting people.

After a person knows about the experience, they can check whether it will work for them. To make the decision to download the TAPP app and ride the bus (or for other experiences, to buy or download the software), the person might use endorsements, reviews, product ratings, and other types of content (Figure 1-4). All of this content helps to get people to the point of commitment.

FIGURE 1-4

For a person investigating whether an experience will work for them, traditional marketing content is appropriate, including ads, product pages, and more. These pieces of content meet the organizational goal of attracting people.

After a person makes the commitment, marketing is over for that person. But the experience still needs to be installed, and the person needs to know how to take their first action (Figure 1-5). *This is where UX content begins.*

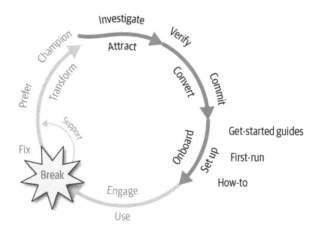

FIGURE 1-5

Onboarding helps people set up the experience. Different experiences might need different kinds of content, from simple first-run experiences to complete get-started guides and how-to information.

Consumer software like the TAPP app can require very little setup: perhaps turning on Location permission, or signing in to buy bus fare. We can write UX text in the first-run experience for our TAPP app so that the first time the person uses the experience, they are able to start meeting their own goals right away.

For software that is being used at work, there's probably more setup required. As a complication, the person who makes the decision to buy software for work is often not the person setting up the software. At a large enough business, an IT pro might need to establish permissions, implement special configurations, or enter data to make the experience work for that business. The organization that made the software can provide UX content for this setup crew, and different UX content for the people who will use the experience day to day.

After the experience is set up, the core UX text takes over. These words are the topic of most of this book. They are the titles, buttons, and descriptions, or voiced comments and instructions from audible experiences that make up half or more of the interactions a person can have with an experience.

If the experience has intrinsic content, like a game, finance, or mapping app, there is special content the person is there for: the game narrative, financial information, and maps. TAPP needs to provide route and timing information as well as bus fare and pass information. To use the experience successfully, people need this content, too (Figure 1-6).

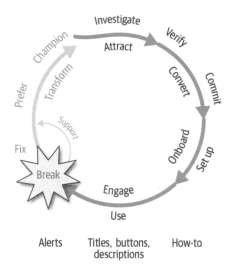

Investigate

Attract

Verify

Champion

Transform

Convert

Commit

Prefer

Onboard

Set up

Support

Fix

Break

Engage

Use

Alerts	Titles, buttons, descriptions	How-to

Game & experience content

FIGURE 1-6

When people are using the experience, they interact with words in titles, buttons, descriptions, and other UX text, plus alerts and other game or consumable content.

How-to content still has a role, whether it's articles in a help center or built in to the UX context. Sometimes, people want a little confidence boost to take their next step. The job of how-to content is to give people that confidence and instruction when they want it.

Sometimes, using the experience doesn't go smoothly. Maybe the TAPP rider has forgotten to update their credit card expiration date, or maybe a bus has been unexpectedly rerouted for an emergency. The organization can use alerts and error messages to inform the person and help them get to their goals (Figure 1-7). The person might seek troubleshooting content, which the organization might provide in a chatbot, or a help center, or on YouTube, or in scripts for support center personnel.

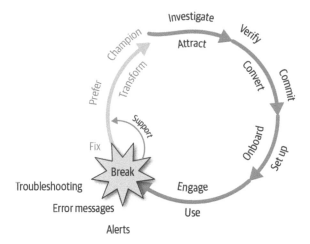

FIGURE 1-7
When there's a break in the experience, the organization can provide error messages, alerts, and troubleshooting content.

Supporting people through a broken experience can make those people into fans of the experience, but there are other ways, too. Giving people badges for different kinds of engagement, and allowing them to get ratings in the experience, means that they have something in this experience that's unique to them that they'd lose if they went to a different experience.

Experiences can also create communities. There are many examples of this: game enthusiasts who join forums to discuss the game, or people who sell on the same online selling platform, or teachers who use a particular classroom management system. Enthusiasts of the experience join forums to share tips and tricks and to be recognized as experts.

Organizations can boost the attractiveness of their experience as well as their brand by providing forums, training, and conferences to give the fans of the experience avenues to attract new people (Figure 1-8).

Considered together, the experiences an organization makes will comprise a huge amount of content (Figure 1-9). That content is a common thread throughout the organization's relationship with the people who buy, set up, use, and hopefully become champions for the experience.

FIGURE 1-8

To give people more reasons to prefer this experience and this organization, the experience can include intrinsic value that isn't available outside of the experience and create communities around the use of the experience to help attract more people into it.

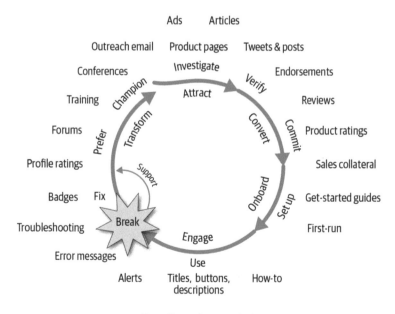

FIGURE 1-9

Examples of content that organizations use to make people aware of their experiences, bring people in, engage them, and reattract them. When the content is designed as a system, the organization benefits.

Today, very few organizations plan their content throughout the cycle. Without the marketing content that attracts and converts people into using the experience, the organization will fail. But, without content for onboarding, engaging, and supporting, the experience will fail to engage and transform those people into champions. UX writing is how we create that content.

Identify Purposes, Opportunities, and Constraints

Writing begins where all design and engineering starts: identifying the purposes, opportunities, and constraints for the experience. Before the writing can begin, the writer needs to identify the goals of the person who will use the experience as well as the goals of the organization making the experience.

To learn the goals for an experience, the writer needs to collaborate with the people who understand and define those goals—the product owner, designer, marketer, researcher, engineer (not an exhaustive list)—and people who will use the experience. From the beginning of ideation and development, the writer needs to participate in the same meetings, discovering and defining the experience in collaboration with their team.

The primary purpose of the text is to meet the goals of the organization and people using the experience, but the text also has a role in protecting both groups. For example, the people using the experience should correctly understand how their data is used and protected. Similarly, the organization needs to have its time, money, and energy protected from liability.

From the beginning, the UX writer needs to know the business constraints, including resources available for localization and the timelines to coordinate engineering and UX content with content for marketing, sales, and support. We also need to know what languages the people using the experience are fluent in, on which devices, and in what contexts. As the experience develops, we need to know technical, display, and design constraints (like maximum URL lengths and text box sizes), which text needs to be coded before hardware is shipped, and which text can be updated from live services.

Writing for UX, just like design and coding for UX, is a design and engineering process. It is an iterative process of creation, measurement, and iteration (Figure 1-10).

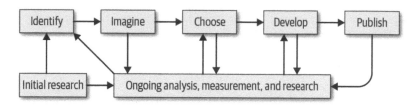

FIGURE 1-10
Writing for UX is an iterative process of creation, measurement, and iteration.

To bring people into the experience, the words need to ground the conversation in what the people who will use it already understand. With the team, the UX writer might conduct foundational, exploratory research about the context for the organization and the person who will use the experience.

In this initial research, the UX writer can listen for sensitive topics that the experience will need to handle with care, including words that have hurtful or offensive connotations. If the experience involves money, health, privacy, or children, it's likely that complex legal or regulatory constraints apply, too. These constraints are essential to understand before designing the voice for the experience.

Now that we know where we want to go, and the tools and limitations we have, we can start the most wildly creative part: imagining how to get there.

Imagine and Test Solutions

For writers, the most creative part of the design and engineering process can be as immersive as play-acting the conversation between the person and the experience, or as straightforward as adapting text that worked in the past for a new situation. But whether blue-sky or mundane, the job is to imagine several distinctly different solutions. By finding many possible solutions, the team can choose the best one to move forward with.

This imagining and testing isn't a solo activity: it's much more difficult to come up with the best breadth of possibilities if you have only yourself to draw from. Even though the UX writer is responsible for marshaling the best ideas for UX content, they are not the only person with great ideas about words. The very best working groups include team members who are familiar with the technical, legal, or financial opportunities and limits, and people who will use the experience. Those people can be experts and novices, enthusiasts or skeptics, fans of the organization, and exclusion experts[1] who are likely to be prevented from using the experience if they aren't included from the beginning.

This working group might participate in formal design activities like a design sprint, brainstorm, or the conversational design exercise that we look at in Chapter 3. They also collaborate informally, in real time and asynchronously. The UX writer participates, bringing their special talent identifying the words and phrases that bring the group together. The writer helps the team discover the different terms they use, drives understanding of the ideas by clarifying words and definitions, and helps articulate the emerging solutions in ways that the entire group understands.

After solutions are imagined, they need to be tested. Understanding what is working and isn't working about the various solutions is vital if the group is going to choose the best solution. From the ongoing research, UX writers learn the words people already use and the phrases that resonate with them. UX writers and UX researchers can collaborate to design questions that elicit the words people would prefer to use.

UX designers need to develop the end-to-end flows, especially for the most common possibilities. The UX writer refines the words by partnering closely with the designers. To ensure the interactions, visual design, and text in the designs work together, we need to draft all of the UX text in the designs. Then, we need to share our best options using tools that the entire team can access.

---

1   In *Mismatch: How Inclusion Shapes Design* (MIT Press, 2018), Kat Holmes defines exclusion experts as "people who experience the greatest mismatch when using your solution, or who might be the most negatively affected."

Writing UX text is iterative, starting with less-than-perfect words, then replacing those words with slightly better words, and repeating until you find the best words. This is the way to make the text purposeful and protective, but also concise, conversational, and recognizable as coming from the organization's brand.

Finally, the team gets ready to launch the experience, feature, or update. Because UX writers can be the single person responsible for stringing words together across all of the screens, they're often one of the very few team members with a broad yet detailed view of the whole experience. The writer can be a big help to their support, marketing, PR, and sales partners, because writers have exact and detailed knowledge of what buttons people need to press and precisely what each error message means.

Summary: Words Make Experiences Work

In this book, I give concrete examples, tools, and advice for the UX writer. But the process isn't always as clear as I've outlined in this chapter. For example, sometimes experiences are developed without clear goals in mind. Sometimes, the UX writer is also the designer, or product owner, or frontend engineer, or marketer. Sometimes, the team (or individual) doesn't make several options, but pursues a single vision. Most teams don't know that there's more that they can do with the words, nor do they know what to do with a writer.

Even if your design and engineering processes aren't ideal, I want to encourage you to consider your options for creating great, strategic UX content. If your organization or team wants to plunge forward without understanding their purpose, OK—but you can identify purposes yourself (voice, Chapter 2). You can imagine brand new text yourself (conversational design, Chapter 3). You can test those options with guerrilla UX research tactics or heuristics, and estimate the impact the final text could make (measurement, Chapter 6). You can advocate for text that is conversational, concise, and purposeful (editing, Chapter 5) and write it faster by taking advantage of text patterns (text patterns, Chapter 4). You can even use the organization's experience success metrics and relate those measurements to the text (measurement, Chapter 6). And if you're just getting started with UX writing for your team, you can socialize the possibilities (30/60/90-day plan, Chapter 8).

[2]

Voice: They Recognize You

They may forget what you said, but they will never forget how you made them feel.
—UNKNOWN, ATTRIBUTED TO MANY

HUMANS ARE AFFECTED BY their interactions and will come away with a feeling they associate with the experiences you create. As the organization responsible for those experiences, we want them to remember how it makes them feel. That feeling makes the experience recognizable, consistent, and distinct from its competitors. *Voice is the set of characteristics that allows content to create that feeling.*

As we saw in Chapter 1, the organization uses content throughout its relationship with people. When the voice is consistent throughout the virtuous cycle, brand affinity is strengthened. People can be more loyal to experiences and organizations that they recognize. Conversely, if we don't design how the content supports that feeling, the person might be left feeling anything: affection, repulsion, loyalty, disgust, or a confusion that leaves them detached.

The biggest barrier to this consistency is the many team members who write the content. Sometimes, they are in different departments in a large organization, and aren't aware of one another. Having a common description of voice helps diverse teams create a cohesive voice.

For example, when I worked at Microsoft in 2010, the voice for the Xbox 360 game system was, "The console speaks like we're sitting beside them, helping them play." The "them" was well understood: console gaming enthusiasts, who just wanted to play their game. How we sat beside them could be further defined: "We're not the guy that takes the controller away and does it himself," which could inspire disgust, disappointment, or frustration, "but the one who will tell you exactly what to do, to make it easy for you," to inspire feelings of camaraderie, achievement, and belonging. Because the gamer and role of the person on the sofa was so familiar to the people making the product, the definition and documentation of voice could be simple.

As Xbox started to understand its broader audience beyond the console gaming enthusiast, we adapted the voice. No matter who was playing or whether they were using the console to watch TV or listen to music, they should have a positive experience. We redefined the voice to be "Clean, casual, and keep 'em playing." We focused the feeling on playing, achievement, and having fun.

These informal descriptions of voice are only as strong as the consistent understanding of that voice. Getting all of the team to understand that description is a major challenge because no team is monolithic. Humans will have different "feelings" for the words. Even speakers of the same language come from different regions and different backgrounds. When multiple teams need to use the same voice, those teams can be working in isolation from one another.

For the change in the Xbox voice, we put up posters in the Xbox buildings to spread the word. We created a special email address so that anybody—from operations to development—could easily reach the dedicated UX writing team for help. The UX writing team used design critiques, hallway brainstorming sessions, and peer reviews of text to stay aligned with one another.

Where there is no UX writing team, the process of developing and aligning the text to the voice has to be managed across the entire organization. Even if responsibility for the text is centered on a single person, that person won't have enough time. UX content will sometimes need to be created without that person. When I faced that challenge at OfferUp, I created a voice chart to define the voice we wanted in a way that anybody at the company could use.

Three Example Experiences

There is a maxim in fiction writing that each character should be recognizable from their dialog: how they speak and what they talk about. It's also a good goal for the voice of an experience that the people using that experience should be able to recognize it from any piece of content.

That way, when a person encounters a message or screen from the organization, they can immediately recognize it, know it's legitimate, and trust it.

To demonstrate, I've invented three different experiences (Figure 2-1), one of which, TAPP, I introduced in Chapter 1:

- The Sturgeon Club, an exclusive club membership app with updates about club events, reservations for facility use, dues paying, menu, and calendar.

- 'appee, a casual social game with daily thematic challenges. Players compete and win prizes by uploading images according to the theme. They also rate other players' images, make comments, and buy items imprinted with images.

- TAPP, a regional bus service web experience with updates per route and region. Riders can find routes, pay fares, and manage their account.

  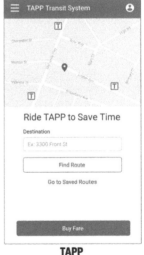

| **The Sturgeon Club** | **'appee** | **TAPP** |
| Social club app with messaging system | Social image-upload game, competing for cash prizes | Transit system app to find routes and pay fare |

FIGURE 2-1
Most examples in this book refer to these fictional experiences: The Sturgeon Club, 'appee, and TAPP.

To be clear, I'm not promoting a design vision with these apps. Their purpose is to demonstrate that within different design choices, the same UX content principles apply. I represent each experience as it might appear on a mobile device, but both The Sturgeon Club and TAPP could easily be web apps.

People who make experiences for people at work, like accounting or IT software, will notice that these are all general-audience, "consumer" experiences. I've chosen these three examples because they allow us to compare some similarities and differences in the UX text. Although there are significant challenges unique to experiences made for work, the patterns and tools in this book apply to both.

In the examples from these experiences throughout this book, my goal is to make the text different enough that even if you didn't see it in context, you could tell which organization it comes from. The UX text in those examples depends on the decisions made in the voice charts created in this chapter. Let's begin!

Creating a Voice Chart

The voice chart (Table 2-1) holds a set of decision-making rules and creative guidance to make the UX content align to the needs of the organization and of the person using the experience. When the UX content is being drafted, the voice chart will help identify what might make it better. When there are multiple good options for the UX content, the voice chart will make deciding between those good options easier. When the UX content is complete, the voice chart will help people move away from subjective judgments and use it as an external success measure (Chapter 6). When there are multiple teammates creating UX content, the voice chart helps them align UX content to the voice. I'll explain how to use it after we build it.

The voice chart shown in Table 2-1 holds each product principle (defined in the next section) in a column. Then, for each principle, each of the six aspects of voice is defined in a different row: the concepts, vocabulary, verbosity, grammar, punctuation, and capitalization.

TABLE 2-1. Blank example voice chart

	PRODUCT PRINCIPLE 1	PRODUCT PRINCIPLE 2	PRODUCT PRINCIPLE 3
Concepts			
Vocabulary			
Verbosity			
Grammar			
Punctuation			
Capitalization			

The definitions in each column relate to the product principle at the top of each column. The definitions in one column aren't expected to be the same as the definitions in another column. It's expected that even in the same row, two columns might contradict or complement each other.

This variation between columns is the difference between *voice* and *tone*. Voice is the consistent, recognizable choice of words across an entire experience. Tone is the variability in that voice from one part of the experience to another. For example, when I overhear my mother answer a phone call, I can quickly tell by her *tone* whether the phone call is from a stranger or a loved one—but I am never confused that it is my mother's *voice*. Similarly, we should be able to recognize an organization or an experience by its voice, even when the tone varies to accommodate, for example, an error message, a notification, or a moment of celebration.

By encapsulating these variations in the same voice chart, the writer is equipped to intentionally include and vary the tone to align the UX content with the overall voice.

In the rest of this chapter, we fill in the voice chart. We begin with the product principles and then tackle the other aspects of voice: concepts, vocabulary, verbosity, grammar, punctuation, and capitalization.

PRODUCT PRINCIPLES

The foundations of the voice chart are the product principles. These principles define what the experience is trying to be to the people who use it. Then, the voice can do its job of conveying those product principles with every word.

To be clear, identifying a product or organization's principles is not usually the job of the UX writer. If your organization has marketing or advertising support, these groups might already have defined these principles. When I have facilitated the articulation of these principles, it has helped me to keep in mind that my goal is not to "own" the product principles, but to align the UX content to them after they are ratified.

When the organization hasn't defined its principles, I recommend interviewing people. In *Nicely Said* (*http://bit.ly/2Xo7wa2*), Nicole Fenton and Kate Kiefer Lee outline a process of interviewing people inside the organization to determine the goals of the brand, the organization, and the experience. If you are fortunate enough to have a UX research partner, this is a great place to enlist their help.

Use the results of interviews to draft the most important principles that emerge and then ratify those with your stakeholders. As the process of refining the product principles continues, the drafts will change considerably—and that's fine. The process of articulating the product principles can become political. When I draft product principles, I expect that the first, second, and even third drafts will end up on the trash heap. The important thing is that the conversations continue, and these early drafts help the stakeholders get to the organization's goal.

For the examples in this book, I've invented three product principles for each organization. Three is not a magic number for product principles; your organization might have more or fewer.

Sturgeon Club

The purpose of the Sturgeon Club is to provide a private, elegant venue for its membership to socialize and recreate. To bring that purpose to life, the club's executive and operations leaders have determined that the physical building, the internal spaces, and each moment the members spend with the club should be imbued with elegance, build camaraderie, and connect members to the club's traditions.

Table 2-2 shows the top row of the voice chart for The Sturgeon Club, which uses each of those three product principles as column headings: Imbued with elegance, Build camaraderie, and Connect to tradition.

TABLE 2-2. The Sturgeon Club voice chart product principles

	IMBUED WITH ELEGANCE	BUILD CAMARADERIE	CONNECT TO TRADITION

'appee

The purpose of 'appee is to create an entertaining, engaging experience for its players while generating content for the platform, engaging with advertising, and buying merchandise. Instead of competing with "serious" art experiences, it is trying a strategy of playfulness, seeking to provide surprising entertainment and moments of insight.

Thus, the 'appee product principles head the columns of its voice chart (Table 2-3): Playful, Insightful, and Surprising.

TABLE 2-3. The 'appee voice chart product principles

	PLAYFUL	INSIGHTFUL	SURPRISING

TAPP

The purpose of the TAPP experience is an extension of the purpose of the regional transit system itself: move people around the region, and therefore through the online experience, in a way the public finds efficient, trustworthy, and accessible. The TAPP voice chart uses those principles as the headings for the principles columns (Table 2-4): Efficient, Trustworthy, and Accessible.

TABLE 2-4. The TAPP voice chart product principles

	EFFICIENT	TRUSTWORTHY	ACCESSIBLE

CONCEPTS

The voice chart helps us to specify, in advance, the concepts that we think will support the product principles. The concepts are the ideas or topics that the organization wants to emphasize at any open opportunity, even when they aren't a part of the task at hand. They are the ideas that reflect the role that the organization wants the experience to have in the person's life.

These concepts don't imply that the experience should endlessly discuss itself and its organizational concerns. Instead, when it can, it includes these ideas. Concepts also don't specify the words to use; they are the ideas that should land regardless of slogans or campaigns.

The Sturgeon Club

The Sturgeon Club voice, for example, specifies to use the details about togetherness and belonging (Table 2-5). For example, instead of describing a formal event space as merely "Capacity of 124 people," the experience could mention "Mingle with up to 124 members."

TABLE 2-5. Concepts aligned to The Sturgeon Club product principles

	IMBUED WITH ELEGANCE	BUILD CAMARADERIE	CONNECT TO TRADITION
Concepts	Details of finish, opulence; functional and ornamental	Togetherness, belonging, and discretion	Specific connections to club members, history, fame, and power

'appee

Concepts included in 'appee are surprising information, small delights, and coincidences (Table 2-6). For example, if 'appee finds that the color blue is featured in a person's high-scoring images, it could choose between messages (both in voice!) of "your blue images score higher" and "some people may be blue, but blue isn't sad for you."

TABLE 2-6. Concepts aligned to 'appee product principles

	PLAYFUL	INSIGHTFUL	SURPRISING
Concepts	Small delights, avoiding grand successes; frippery	Commonalities found especially at the intersection of ideas	Unpredictable; misdirection and difficulty can be fun

TAPP

The TAPP experience adds very few new concepts to the experience. If they are included, they are specific to supporting the operating principles: a lack of waste, rides happening on time, and the inclusion of every possible rider (Table 2-7). For example, TAPP might indicate "98% on time" for a bus route at a particular stop.

TABLE 2-7. Concepts aligned to TAPP product principles

	EFFICIENT	TRUSTWORTHY	ACCESSIBLE
Concepts	Waste no resource	Every ride on time	Rides for every rider

VOCABULARY

Where specific words can support or undermine a voice principle, use the Vocabulary row to specify them. If there aren't specific words that help land the principle, you can omit this row.

This vocabulary row doesn't replace a robust *word list* or *terminology list.* A word list is a traditional part of a style guide to define spelling and usage choices like "canceled" versus "cancelled." A terminology list defines the words that are given meanings specific to the experience. In comparison, this vocabulary row in the voice chart specifies only the few words that are so important to the experience that they help identify its personality.

The Sturgeon Club

The Sturgeon Club vocabulary serves to reinforce the social order (Table 2-8). A member might have an *appointment* with staff such as a nutritionist or concierge. But members *meet* with one another. Generalities are to be avoided, and so is referring to someone as a "former member."

TABLE 2-8. Vocabulary aligned to The Sturgeon Club product principles

	IMBUED WITH ELEGANCE	BUILD CAMARADERIE	CONNECT TO TRADITION
Vocabulary	Avoid generalities ("very," "really," etc.)	Secure, not safe meet with members appointment with staff	member member emeritus, member (deceased), not former member

'appee

Vocabulary isn't the same kind of tool in 'appee as it is in The Sturgeon Club. In Table 2-9, Playful and Surprising don't specify any vocabulary to use or avoid. Even in the one place it does reference vocabulary, it is vague but important: Use plain, nonmetaphoric descriptions, such as "Your Wednesday photos are your best photos."

TABLE 2-9. Vocabulary aligned to 'appee product principles

	PLAYFUL	INSIGHTFUL	SURPRISING
Vocabulary	{not terminology specific}	Plain, nonmetaphoric descriptions	{not terminology specific}

TAPP

In Table 2-10, the TAPP voice chart specifies words that could be used throughout the experience. Notably, the Accessible principle says to never use "disabled" or "invalid," but encourages the use of "available," "easy," and "ready." In practice, this means that the team avoids words that can exclude people who use wheelchairs and other assistive devices; instead, it includes them by specifying what is and isn't available, easy, or ready.

TABLE 2-10. Vocabulary aligned to TAPP product principles

	EFFICIENT	TRUSTWORTHY	ACCESSIBLE
Vocabulary	Fast, save time, save money	regular, on time	available, easy, ready Never use: disabled, invalid

VERBOSITY

For strict usability, the words inside an experience should get out of people's way. The UX text isn't there to be savored or read for pleasure. But using few words where many are expected can block a person from moving forward as thoroughly as using too many words where few are expected. Screen size and reading format makes a difference, too: people are more willing to read on a desktop computer or mobile device than on a TV screen.

The Sturgeon Club

The Sturgeon Club intentionally sets a measured pace. It is not afraid to take time to expand upon its own glory, so it will enhance descriptions with adjectives and adverbs (Table 2-11). The club also wants an air of formality, even where a more casual atmosphere is common, so it will use complete sentences (and therefore more words), even where people would usually use short phrases. However, there is a tension between setting a stately pace and wasting the members' time: members are there to build camaraderie with one another, not with the concierge, the staff, or the experience.

TABLE 2-11. Verbosity aligned to The Sturgeon Club product principles

	IMBUED WITH ELEGANCE	BUILD CAMARADERIE	CONNECT TO TRADITION
Verbosity	Enhance responses and descriptions with adjectives/adverbs	Be brief and begone; they aren't here to talk to the concierge	Complete sentences even where phrases are more common

'appee

'appee demonstrates playfulness with its entry for Playful on the Verbosity row of its voice chart (Table 2-12). As a casual game, 'appee needs to introduce difficulty or challenge in the use of the game. One way it can do this is by using fewer words than strictly necessary to get its point across. This cell in the 'appee voice chart is a good reminder that the voice for any experience is used like a spice when cooking: too little and the food is unappetizing; too much, and the food is inedible. If the UX writer applied this part of the voice too heavily, there would be no words in the experience at all!

TABLE 2-12. Verbosity aligned to 'appee product principles

	PLAYFUL	INSIGHTFUL	SURPRISING
Verbosity	Fewer ~~than strictly necessary~~	{not verbosity specific}	{not verbosity specific}

TAPP

The Verbosity row of the TAPP voice chart exhorts the team to avoid unnecessary adjectives or adverbs, except to ensure the person's success, to be accurate, and to be unambiguous (Table 2-13). As a public service, the TAPP voice aligns neatly with its utilitarian purpose.

TABLE 2-13. Verbosity aligned to TAPP product principles

	EFFICIENT	TRUSTWORTHY	ACCESSIBLE
Verbosity	No adjectives or adverbs except to ensure rider success	Enough words to have accurate information	Enough words to have unambiguous information

GRAMMAR

Natural language gives us a rich variety of ways to construct and convey our ideas, but all of those ways don't work in all experiences. To maximize usability, simple grammatical structures work best for most purposes. In English, this means that simple subject-predicate sentences, or verb-object imperative directions such as "The bus accepts correct change and transit passes" and "Add money to your transit pass."

However, merely maximizing usability can result in a robotic, impersonal tone. By choosing the sentence structures and other grammar that support the product principles, you have an opportunity to define the right balance of usability and personality for the experience.

The Sturgeon Club

The Sturgeon Club reinforces its culture in its use of the Grammar row of its voice chart (Table 2-14). To imbue elegance, the experience should consider complex sentence structures. But to build camaraderie, the simple grammar is preferred for discussing people. Most important, the club itself is spoken of in the grammar associated with formality: passive voice, past tense, and complex sentences.

TABLE 2-14. Grammar aligned to The Sturgeon Club product principles

	IMBUED WITH ELEGANCE	BUILD CAMARADERIE	CONNECT TO TRADITION
Grammar	In descriptions of experience, prefer complex to simple or compound	When discussing people, prefer simple statements	When discussing the club, prefer passive voice, past tense, complex and compound sentences

'appee

In contrast to The Sturgeon Club, 'appee prefers using the present and future tense. Even when it presents its rules, it doesn't use complete sentences (Chapter 3, Figure 3-9), as specified by the Grammar row of its voice chart (Table 2-15).

TABLE 2-15. Grammar aligned to 'appee product principles

	PLAYFUL	INSIGHTFUL	SURPRISING
Grammar	Present and future tense	{not grammar specific}	Phrases preferred

TAPP

TAPP continues its utilitarian style in the Grammar row of its voice chart (Table 2-16). It uses complete sentences to emphasize trustworthiness, but phrases are also acceptable, as long as they are simple.

TABLE 2-16. Grammar aligned to TAPP product principles

	EFFICIENT	TRUSTWORTHY	ACCESSIBLE
Grammar	Simple sentences or phrases	Complete sentences	Simple sentences or phrases

PUNCTUATION AND CAPITALIZATION

There is a strong argument to be made that punctuation and capitalization are part of the visual and typographic design of experience and are not the responsibility of the UX writer. This is where most style guides do their heavy lifting: when to use commas, how to use en dashes, and more. As a starting point, the organization might choose to use an established style guide: AP, *Modern Language Association*, *Chicago Manual of Style*, and APA styles, to name a few.

Regardless of how the style is chosen or who owns those decisions in an organization, punctuation and capitalization continue to be among the most frequent bugs I get about UX text. One of the purposes of the voice chart is to have the discussions and record the result so that future confusion can be avoided, and the experience can be made consistent.

The Sturgeon Club

The Sturgeon Club voice chart details how capitalization emphasizes relationships and roles within the club (Table 2-17). It also emphasizes commas and eschews exclamation marks and tildes.

TABLE 2-17. Punctuation and capitalization aligned to The Sturgeon Club product principles

	IMBUED WITH ELEGANCE	BUILD CAMARADERIE	CONNECT TO TRADITION
Punctuation	Serial commas, colon instead of em dash, no tilde, and no exclamation mark.	{not punctuation specific}	Sentences include terminal punctuation. Titles do not.
Capitalization	Title case is used for titles, buttons, headings	Relationship roles (friend, spouse, parent) are not capitalized	Member titles, roles, committee titles, names, and roles are initial-capitalized

'appee

'appee enjoys fringe punctuation, preferring to stretch into playfulness away from tradition and formality. Instead of using capitalization to signify importance, it indicates that capitalization should be used only for emphasis (Table 2-18).

TABLE 2-18. Punctuation and capitalization aligned to 'appee product principles

	PLAYFUL	INSIGHTFUL	SURPRISING
Punctuation	Avoid periods; use emoji, exclamations, interrobangs, question marks	Tilde instead of colon, semicolon, dash, or ellipsis	{not punctuation specific}
Capitalization	Use capitalization only for emphasis	Use sentence case	{not capitalization specific}

TAPP

With its Punctuation and Capitalization rows in its voice chart (Table 2-19), TAPP focuses on clarity as the best route to efficiency, trustworthiness, and accessibility. TAPP uses commas and periods, and avoids semicolons, dashes, parenthetical remarks, and question marks. Titles and buttons are immediately recognizable as members of a hierarchy because of their capitalization.

TABLE 2-19. Punctuation and capitalization aligned to TAPP product principles

	EFFICIENT	TRUSTWORTHY	ACCESSIBLE
Punctuation	Use periods, commas. Avoid question marks. Avoid terminal punctuation for instructions	Use periods, commas. Avoid question marks. Avoid terminal punctuation for instructions	Avoid semicolons, dashes, parenthetical remarks
Capitalization	Title-case titles, headings, buttons	Title-case titles, headings, buttons	Title-case titles, headings, buttons

COMPLETING THE VOICE CHART

With all of the rows put together, the voice chart is a formidable tool to keep the UX content focused on meeting the goals of the organization and the people who will use the experience. Each content decision can be informed and aligned to be in the same voice, no matter who is writing that content.

When defined like this, the team can identify natural points of conflict within the voice. For example, 'appee specifies nonmetaphoric descriptions for its insights, but also to be unpredictable and use fewer words than necessary. In the imagining process outlined in the next section, I demonstrate how to use these tensions within the voice chart to imagine broadly different solutions and how to choose among them.

Tables 2-20, 2-21, and 2-22 present the complete voice charts for The Sturgeon Club, 'appee, and TAPP, respectively.

TABLE 2-20. The complete voice chart for The Sturgeon Club

	ELEGANCE	CAMARADERIE	TRADITION
Concepts	Details of finish, opulence; functional and ornamental	Togetherness, belonging, and discretion	Specific connections to club members, history, fame, and power
Vocabulary	Avoid generalities ("very," "really," etc.)	Secure, not safe meet with members appointment with staff	member member emeritus, member (deceased), not former member
Verbosity	Enhance responses and descriptions with adjectives/adverbs	Be brief and begone; they aren't here to talk to the concierge	Complete sentences even where phrases are more common
Grammar	In descriptions of experience, prefer complex to simple or compound	When discussing people, prefer simple statements	When discussing the club, prefer passive voice, past tense, complex and compound sentences
Punctuation	Serial commas, colon instead of em dash, no tilde, and no exclamation mark.	{not punctuation specific}	Sentences include terminal punctuation. Titles do not.
Capitalization	Title case is used for titles, buttons, headings	Relationship roles (friend, spouse, parent) are not capitalized	Member titles, roles, committee titles, names, and roles are initial-capitalized

TABLE 2-21. The complete voice chart for 'appee

	PLAYFUL	INSIGHTFUL	SURPRISING
Concepts	Small delights, avoiding grand successes; frippery	Commonalities found especially at the intersection of ideas	Unpredictable; misdirection and difficulty can be fun
Vocabulary	{not vocabulary specific}	Plain, nonmetaphoric descriptions	{not vocabulary specific}
Verbosity	Fewer ~~than strictly necessary~~	{not verbosity specific}	{not verbosity specific}
Grammar	Present and future tense	Slogans over observations	Phrases preferred
Punctuation	Avoid periods; use emoji, exclamations, interrobangs, question marks	Tilde instead of colon, semicolon, dash, or ellipsis	{not punctuation specific}
Capitalization	Use capitalization only for emphasis	Use sentence case	{not capitalization specific}

TABLE 2-22. The complete voice chart for TAPP

	EFFICIENT	TRUSTWORTHY	ACCESSIBLE
Concepts	Waste no resource	Every ride on time	Rides for every rider
Vocabulary	Fast, save time, save money	regular, on time	available, easy, ready
Verbosity	No adjectives or adverbs except to ensure rider success	Enough words to have accurate information	Enough words to have unambiguous information
Grammar	Simple sentences or phrases	Complete sentences	Simple sentences or phrases
Punctuation	Use periods, commas. Avoid question marks. Avoid terminal punctuation for instructions	Use periods, commas. Avoid question marks. Avoid terminal punctuation for instructions	Avoid semicolons, dashes, parenthetical remarks
Capitalization	Title-case titles, headings, buttons	Title-case titles, headings, buttons	Title-case titles, headings, buttons

To understand how voice helps make an experience recognizable, consider the sign-in screens for The Sturgeon Club, 'appee, and TAPP side by side (Figure 2-2).

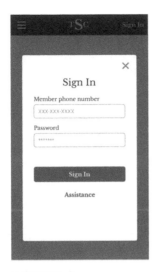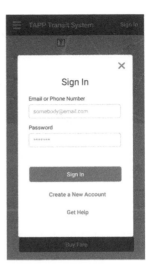

FIGURE 2-2

Sign-in screens for all three example apps illustrate their differences in voice.
You can find more examples of each voice in Chapter 4.

Note that the design system for each experience is nearly identical, but
the text differences create recognizable differences. The Sturgeon Club
specifies "Member phone number" and offers "Assistance." 'appee
uses fewer words than necessary by deciding not to offer labels for the
text entry fields (a difficult choice for usability). TAPP creates the most
accessible experience it can, with unambiguous, complete labels and
buttons.

Using the Voice Chart as a Decision-Making and Iteration Tool

To make the voice chart authoritative in the organization, it must be ratified by parties at the highest level possible in the organization. It will
need their sponsorship and support for the team to be aware of it and to
take it seriously enough to realize its value in their own work.

Plan the ceremony of a high-level sign-off. Ceremonies and unveilings
are how organizations indicate their level of investment in an idea. To
be effective and visible as a decision-making tool, the voice chart needs
that investment.

In the meeting, walk decision makers through the voice chart, piece by piece. Provide before-and-after examples of content that can be made better by rewriting it for alignment. Demonstrate how you will use the voice chart to inform decisions and how you will measure its effect on sentiment, engagement, or other metrics relevant to your organization (see Chapter 6).

Plan a second meeting for leaders to present the voice chart to the team, and follow up by driving awareness in newsletters, email announcements, or other channels appropriate to the team's culture.

After the voice chart is adopted by the organization, it's time to use it as a tool to make decisions and make improvements. The voice chart has three main roles: training new UX writers, designing new text, and breaking ties.

TRAINING NEW CONTENT CREATORS

One of the things a UX writer needs to do when they join the team is to internalize the ideas, vocabulary, and grammar that the experience uses strategically. The voice chart gives them a structured reference to learn that voice in the same way they learn any other aspect of the organization.

Feedback from others is especially helpful to onboard new team members. Using the voice chart to ground that feedback can help them to learn faster. For example, "Our voice is to use the simplest possible grammar. Is there a way to make it simpler?" Or, "Could you add more about this concept, given that it's part of our voice?"

IMAGINING

Use the voice chart when designing new UX text. Choose one of the product principles that applies to the moment in the experience, and draft the UX text to amplify that principle. Then, putting aside that option, repeat that drafting process with a second product principle, using those different ideas, vocabulary, and grammar.

For example, the TAPP product principles are Efficient, Trustworthy, and Accessible. The main screen of the TAPP experience includes a map with the person's location, a search box to find a transit route, and a main button to buy or pay bus fare.

The title needs to introduce the TAPP value and promise and not distract from the main actions the person will take, either to find a route or to buy a bus fare. By using the voice chart to guide the iterations, I've created three versions of the title, one aligned to each of the three principles (Figure 2-3).

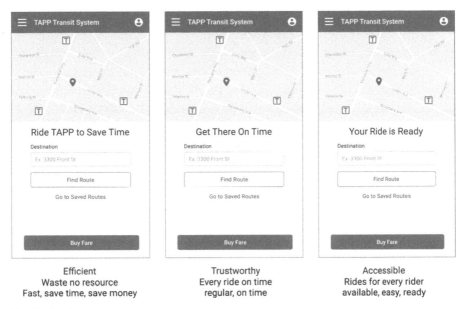

FIGURE 2-3
The main screen of the TAPP Transit System experience, with different possible headlines to align to each of the TAPP principles.

By creating versions of the content that align to different product principles, each of which are a part of the brand, we're exercising the content. The UX text becomes capable of lifting more weight and is more capable of meeting its purpose when we have a clear articulation of that purpose and how we intend to meet it. That's what the voice chart is for.

For any set of text, this iterative process will give you a broader range of options to choose from. The more very different, very good options you can share with your team, the more you will change the conversation from "we need to fix the words" to "let's find and test the best options." Then, it's time to decide which of the good options to use.

DECISION MAKING AND TIE BREAKING

When you have created several good options for the UX text, you have multiple good options you can test against one another to determine the difference in their effectiveness (read more in Chapter 6 about testing and measurement).

When testing isn't possible, practical, or desirable, usually the UX writer and the team can nominate one of the options as their favorite. When there are disagreements about which option to use, breaking a tie will come down to how your organization makes decisions. There are three common methods that I've seen in teams and organizations: consensus, autonomous decisions, and hierarchical decisions:

Consensus decisions

> When an organization has a preference for driving consensus, make the case for the best option. Frame your argument by illustrating the problems to be solved, including both the immediate needs and the broader organizational objectives. Use the voice chart to remind the group about the need of the organization to build the brand's relationship with the people who will use the experience.

Autonomous decisions

> When an organization prefers independent, responsible work, the choice might be all up to you! In addition to seeking feedback from others, use the chart as your own personal checklist: does the text include the right ideas? Is it phrased according to the predefined grammar? If you have two great options for voice and usability, either of them will work. You can literally flip a coin.

Hierarchical or autocratic decisions

> In many organizations, people higher in the hierarchy are the designated decision makers, regardless of who holds specific knowledge or expertise. The decision makers want to make the best possible choice, both for the organization and the team, so they will seek information from their experts and networks. In the ideal situation, the decision maker trusts their experts; otherwise, their decision-making powers can't scale. By consulting with their experts and networks about the benefits and risks of the options, the decision maker and the organization can have more confidence in their decision.

If the option preferred by the decision maker isn't aligned to the voice, the voice chart itself can serve as a tie breaker. Because you did the work to have the voice chart ratified, it holds the same authority as the highest-level person who signed off on it. For example, a team that disagrees with the voice needs to have a rationale that will convince the CEO, if the voice was signed off by the CEO.

Summary: Lift Every Voice

The voice of an experience is made up of many choices in the text. It begins with the ideas we choose to include or exclude, even if those words don't have a detectable difference on the "doing" at hand. It continues with the words we choose, how many we use, how we organize them, and how we use punctuation and capitalization.

When we create the voice of an experience with intention, we can use word choices as a power tool to align every word to the goals of the organization and the customer. But it's not a one-person tool: creating the voice chart is work that will take time and investment from a broad set of stakeholders.

Even if a UX writer is certain that they could create the voice chart in isolation, they should resist the temptation. The minimum team to establish the voice will include representatives from marketing, research, product, leadership, support, and design. The experience will reflect the people who make it, so we can create greater and more scalable future success by shepherding the team through the process of defining how the product principles affect the voice. To get people speaking in the new voice, they will need to consider it, commit to it, and practice it. Together, the team can use the voice chart to create the feelings that people are seeking, and better create the success that the organization needs.

Creating those feelings with UX content starts by writing the words that people will experience. In the next three chapters, we dive into practical techniques for writing, editing, and measuring those words.

[3]

Conversation for Content-First Design

The role of the designer is that of a good, thoughtful host anticipating the needs of his guests.

—CHARLES EAMES, AMERICAN DESIGNER

Writing from scratch is daunting when the page is blank, the sky is blue, and the task is described only as "make something entertaining." But that's not what UX writers are for. Our words aren't there to be read, savored, and appreciated, but to pass unremembered while they help get somebody to the thing they want. When we approach UX writing, we know where we start: the goals of the organization and of the people who will use the experience, and the work we've already done to determine the voice.

In this chapter, I share an exercise based on the primary way humans interact with others: *the conversation*. It's a method of designing an experience that starts before the diagrams or screens. (For existing UX text, try Chapter 5.)

Conversation is somehow in our genetic makeup. Humans take turns speaking and responding in ways that cross languages, continents, and cultures.[1] Conversation is a lot older than responding to pixels on screens and sounds from speakers, so it still governs how we respond to those pixels and sounds.

Throughout this book, when I write that UX text should be *conversational*, I am not specifying a voice or tone, like "casual conversation" or "folksy." I mean that it is recognizable to humans as an interaction they are having with the words. When a person is interacting with the experience, they are in conversation with it.

---

1   *How We Talk: The Inner Workings of Conversation* by N.J. Enfield (Basic Books, 2017).

At the beginning of a new design process, we can lead with content when we start with goals (everything starts with goals!), create the conversation, and create wireframe designs from there.

Face-to-Face, Full-Body Design

In this exercise, you work through the experience as if it were a face-to-face conversation. You'll need to have an idea of the place people will start from, when they use the experience, and what they want. You'll also need to know why the organization wants this interaction to happen. In its best circumstance, you'll have one or more people to create these designs with, which is how I'll describe the process.

To prepare for conversational design, collect some sticky notes, a whiteboard, and markers (or other shareable way to take notes). Gather your partner or small group; none of the group is required to be a dedicated UX writer, but all of them should have some familiarity with the organization and the people who will use the experience.

The best kind of group to assemble will include representatives of the core stakeholders for both the organization and the people who will use the experience. For your organization, that might be team members from design, research, product, business, and engineering. For the people who will use the experience, variety is key: you want people who can represent the breadth of the humans that your experience will try to serve. They can be people new to the experience, people who already use it, people who use similar experiences easily, and people who are excluded from similar experiences.

Note what you don't need: you don't need designs and you don't need screens. You want to avoid thinking about the design elements that you could use to represent the conversation. All of that will come later.

In this example, we examine how to renew a bus pass with TAPP. Begin by identifying where the person is coming from and what outcome the person wants. Put these starting and ending places on a wall or whiteboard that the entire small group can use, at either end of a long arrow (Figure 3-1). The rest of the conversation will go in the middle.

FIGURE 3-1
At the beginning of a conversational design exercise, start with the person's intention at the beginning of a long arrow, and the result they want at the other end of the arrow.

Next, with the participation of the small group, make lists to answer two questions:

- Why is the person in this experience; why are they doing this thing?

- Why does this organization provide this experience?

Write the answers to these questions with the same long arrow so that they can be referred to and updated during the exercise (Figure 3-2).

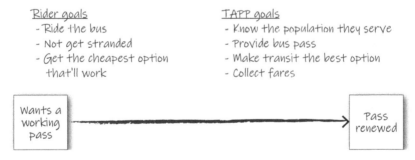

FIGURE 3-2
To inform the conversation exercise, add two lists to the long arrow: the goals of people using the experience, and the goals of the organization.

Now that the basics are in place, it's time to role play. People in your small group will act out two roles: one, the person using the experience, and two, the experience itself. This is similar to improvisation techniques used in theater, but you don't need to perform for an audience. You'll only save the best parts to create the experience.

The best way to role play is to get up and move. By letting body language do some of the talking, the team will uncover nuances of the conversation that will make a better experience. For example, if the experience involves a purchase, set up the physical scene for success by having the "organization" stand behind a counter, like a faux cashier. If you're working on the first-run or onboarding experience, start on opposite sides of a closed door, and let the person knock on the door to enter.

The job of the person using the experience is to make it clear what they want and to keep pushing toward that outcome in a way that will meet their goals.

The job of the person role playing the experience is to help the person achieve the outcome they're looking for while meeting the organization's goals. The person experience is the thoughtful host, anticipating the needs of the person using the experience. Together, they will improvise a conversation and then iterate it until the conversation meets all of their goals.

After the actors are physically in place, the person playing the organization starts the conversation. "What can I help you with?" is a pretty good place to begin (even if you decide to change that start later).

Each person should have an opportunity to be the experience and the person who uses the experience. A best practice is to vary the kinds of people who are represented, including different needs and different capabilities. By taking turns, each person should also play the experience.

Unless you have a team that has practiced improvisation, this process might feel awkward the first few times. *Stick with it.* I recommend getting through the conversation at least twice before pausing the first time. If any role player becomes stuck, they should refer to the list of goals and outcomes. When all of the goals and outcomes are met, for both parties, they can end the experience.

Each time the conversation is acted, record the topics on the arrow diagram you've already started (Figure 3-3). Write the topics in the order in which they happened between the two endpoints. When people come up with great phrases to explain a concept or ask a question, write those down.

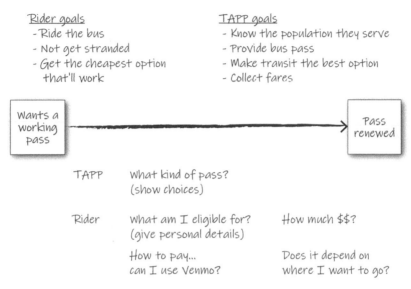

FIGURE 3-3
Rough notes, including the phrases and sequence of the conversation, are drawn where they appear on the arrow between the two endpoints.

As a team, you can consider and role play the following: what would happen if you asked the questions in a different order? What would happen if you asked them in a different way? What if the person were a child, or a person who needed something more or less complex? This exercise is your laboratory to test those ideas.

By intentionally sequencing the topics, you make the experience more effective and more enjoyable. It also helps to raise terminology to the surface and introduce what terms might need to be defined, rethought, or specifically introduced.

At this phase the conversation will be pretty messy, and that's one of the points of this exercise. These diagrams give you the starting draft for the design work that will follow.

Transforming the Conversation into an Experience

After the team has played the conversation through several explorations, it's time to record what you have come up with. Take pictures of the messy version, in case you need to refer to it later. But also distill the messy version into a clean version that you all agree on, like the row of notes on the arrow in Figure 3-4.

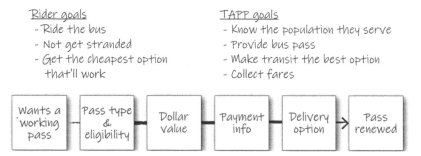

Rider goals
- Ride the bus
- Not get stranded
- Get the cheapest option
  that'll work

TAPP goals
- Know the population they serve
- Provide bus pass
- Make transit the best option
- Collect fares

| Wants a working pass | Pass type & eligibility | Dollar value | Payment info | Delivery option | Pass renewed |

FIGURE 3-4

The rough notes of the conversation exercise are distilled into a sequence of notes, sometimes called a "user journey," that meets the goals of the people and the organization.

Next, it's time to see what the words look like when written down. Some spoken words, although common and conversational, aren't easy to read. One way to write it is as a text message conversation, using side-by-side text bubbles (Figure 3-5).

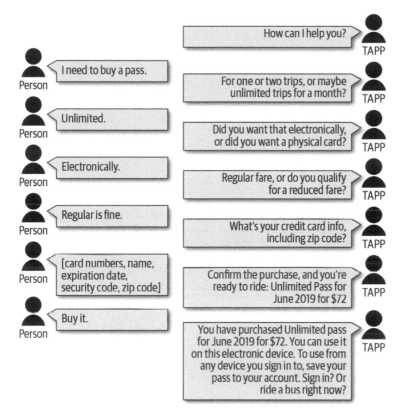

FIGURE 3-5

A refinement of the conversation between TAPP and a person who wants to buy a bus pass using side-by-side text message bubbles.

At the end of the conversational design exercise, you have a design for the overall conversation. You know when key terminology needs to be introduced, and you have draft text that you can use to get started.

The UX or interaction designer has enough to wireframe a visual experience, to start mapping a voice interface experience, or to create a physical, in-person experience. The phrases said by the experience will become the titles, labels, and descriptions. The phrases said by the person will become the buttons and options they choose within the experience.

An initial wireframe of buying a TAPP pass, using content-first design, might look like Figure 3-6.

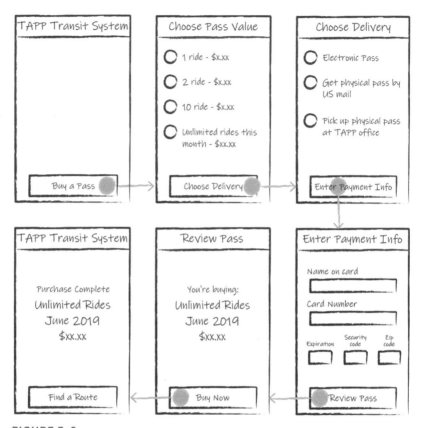

FIGURE 3-6

The results of the conversational design exercise: an initial wireframe of buying a bus pass in TAPP, representing all six steps.

In the exercise, the team might identify entry points to additional experiences (in this TAPP example, to sign in or ride the bus). They'll also uncover edge cases and error situations like expired credit cards. These can be documented with the design so that the experience feels like a cohesive whole.

Summary: Now You're Having the Right Conversation

The UX text and design aren't optimized, but you have accomplished the most difficult, most essential work: the conversation. The team knows the experience will be aligned to the goals for both the organization and the people who will use it. The team can be confident that the right conversation will happen.

But the work is not complete! Now that the conversation exists, the UX writer can refine the UX text according to placement, scannability, and voice. This single path can be widened and forked according to the different needs and circumstances of the people who will use the experience. The UX writer can go straight to the iterative editing process or get a jump start with those edits by applying UX text patterns.

[4]

Apply UX Text Patterns

Pay attention to the intricate patterns of your existence that you take for granted.
—DOUG DILLON, WRITER

A design pattern is a reusable, common solution to a design problem. The goal of this set of UX text patterns is to establish an easy, recognizable starting place to write consistently high-quality text. They are a tool to quickly and scalably write new UX text based on text patterns that have been successful in the past.

Like other good design patterns, these patterns don't prescribe the words to use. They also shouldn't create the impression that the pattern is necessary to solve any particular problem; sometimes, UX text isn't the appropriate solution at all.

The UX text patterns included here are a basic set that almost every experience must use:

- Titles
- Buttons and other interactive text
- Descriptions
- Empty states
- Labels
- Controls
- Text input fields
- Transitional text
- Confirmation messages
- Notifications
- Errors

For each of the UX text patterns in this chapter, I provide three pieces of critical information: the pattern's purpose, definition, and use. I also provide examples of each pattern using the book's example experiences: The Sturgeon Club, 'appee, and TAPP. This way, you can see a variety of text patterns in different voices.

To help keep the examples clear, The Sturgeon Club screens are on the left side, 'appee screens in the middle, and TAPP screens are on the right side of their respective figures. Each experience is shown as a mobile app for illustration purposes, but the same UX text patterns apply to desktop and TV screen experiences.

Let's begin with the first piece of content encountered in most experiences: the title.

Titles

Purpose: Provide immediate clarity of context and action to be taken.

A title is a label that indicates the top levels of hierarchy in the information architecture. Titles are frequently the first and only text a person reads in an experience. That means that for the person to be successful, the title needs to provide context.

There are at least four good ways to set that context, depending on where it occurs in the experience. Here are the four kinds of title I describe:

- Brand name
- Content name
- Ambiguous task
- Single task

BRAND-NAME TITLE

At moments in the experience that define the brand, the context to set is the experience itself. Use the name of the experience to set that context, as a brand-name title.

For example, the main screen of The Sturgeon Club uses the club monogram and name as the brand-name title (Figure 4-1). This is the screen each member of The Sturgeon Club experience would encounter most often, and it should convey the recognizable brand.

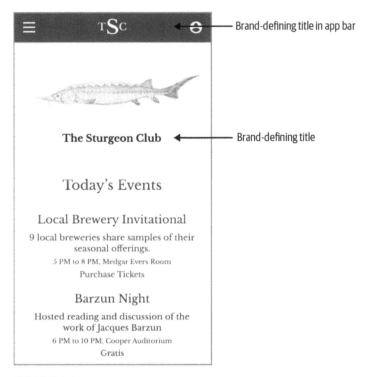

FIGURE 4-1
Brand-name titles on the main screen of The Sturgeon Club experience.

Many apps use the very top of the screen for a title relevant to the screen, but not The Sturgeon Club. Part of what the club provides for its members is the feeling of belonging to the club itself, so The Sturgeon Club has committed to having a persistent monogram, its brand, acting as a title for every screen.

On the body of the screen, The Sturgeon Club reinforces the information hierarchy with a second brand-name title. By including both titles on the main page, the experience subtly sets the expectation that each screen will set its own context within the page.

CONTENT-NAME TITLE

When a screen is based on content, such as a blog post, social media post, or image, the screen might use a title based on that content: the content-name title. These content name titles can be specified by the person who created the content, like the publisher of a blog, or it can be generated from the content itself, like the titles generated for single posts on social media.

For example, 'appee uses the name of the challenge as the title for every image submitted for that challenge. For the 'appee screen that shows the Grand Prize winner for the Bluster challenge, the appropriate title is "Bluster" (Figure 4-2).

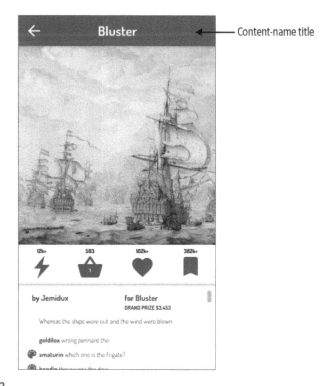

FIGURE 4-2

'appee uses the name of the challenge as the title for every image submitted for that challenge. In this figure, the winner for the Bluster challenge has the content name title "Bluster" in the app bar.

AMBIGUOUS-TASKS TITLE

On screens with multiple potential actions that the person can take, like a dashboard view of a person's account, it's helpful to use a title that covers the entire set of ambiguous tasks.

For these ambiguous-tasks titles, use a noun or noun phrase that names the person's context, or a verb phrase that indicates the relevant category of actions that they can take. The title can reassure the person that they are in the right place to accomplish their goal, even though the experience doesn't know which goal the person has in mind.

For example, there are many possible reasons a player might view their own profile screen in the 'appee experience. The person might want to browse their past photos, review their stats, or update their profile photo or other details. Therefore, the title (Figure 4-3) is the descriptive phrase "how you look." Because the person could have more than one account, it's also important to indicate who "you" is. 'appee solves that problem by using a content-name title on the screen.

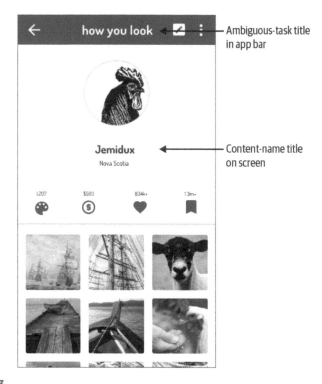

FIGURE 4-3

When 'appee player Jemidux opens their profile in the 'appee experience, they encounter the ambiguous-tasks title "how you look" and their player name as the content-name title of the screen.

SINGLE-TASK TITLE

Single-task titles act as instructions for the person to take an action. Use an imperative verb phrase as a direction to reinforce the correct action.

For example, in Figure 4-4, the TAPP experience displays the code a person must scan when they get on the bus, to pay for their ride. The TAPP experience uses the single-task title "Pay Fare." There is no button to use to take that action; the person must take the next action using the code-reader on the bus.

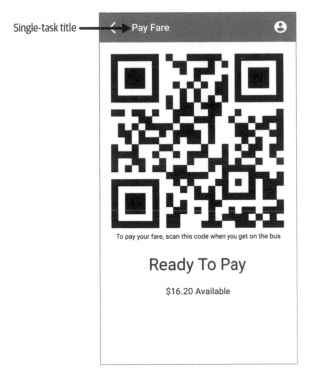

Single-task title → ‹ Pay Fare

To pay your fare, scan this code when you get on the bus

Ready To Pay

$16.20 Available

FIGURE 4-4
The Pay Fare screen in the TAPP experience has a single-task title in the app bar.

Titles, however they are used, are just the starting place. The real action takes place when people interact with the text by tapping, clicking, or otherwise selecting it.

As the single-task title demonstrates, the title's main purpose is frequently to introduce the action that the person can take. Most of the time, they will take that action by using a button.

Buttons, Links, and Other Commands

Purpose: Allow the person to advance toward or commit to action.

Buttons and other interactive text are any text that a person interacts with by tapping, clicking, or speaking to get to their next step. Sometimes they are called *links, calls to action,* or *commands,* but whether they are performing an action, taking the person to the next screen, or navigating elsewhere, we will consider them together in this pattern.

Buttons are some of the most important text in an experience. They are how the person makes their purpose known. Buttons (and to a limited extent, controls) are how people "speak" to the experience. The button must be used to enable the conversation between the person and the experience. Almost every other piece of text, from title, description, empty state, label, confirmation, error, and more, is the experience speaking to the person.

The challenge of buttons is that they work best when they are recognizable, specific, and only one or two words long. In experiences I have tested, buttons that are one or two words long were more frequently used than any buttons longer than two words. Similarly, buttons that used a word that the person would actually say in a conversation outperformed generic buttons and buttons with words the person wouldn't have chosen.

For example, when someone wants to review and pay their club charges in The Sturgeon Club, they encounter the Folio screen (Figure 4-5). The button "Pay $308.48" is the button most important to the club because this is its revenue stream. The text is a clear verb-first indicator of action. Putting the amount to pay on the same button makes it even more specific. Because the member already has a payment method registered in the experience, the payment can be completed with this single, seamless action.

There are two other options available to The Sturgeon Club member: the verb-first command of Change Payment Method, and the back arrow. The order of the buttons is important: just like they would be in a conversation, the most common or primary action would be brought up first.

Folio

Prepared July 8, 2019

Membership Dues	
July 2019 Dues	$250.00
Paid Automatically	-$250.00

Events	
July 4 Gala Extraordinaire	$50.00
Charity Raffle Tickets	$20.00
Auction Purchase	$120.00
Juneteenth Celebration	No Charge
Charity Raffle Tickets	$20.00

Dining

Change Payment Method ◄———— Verb-first command

Pay $308.48 ◄———— Verb-first command, specifying payment amount

FIGURE 4-5

When reviewing and paying their charges in The Sturgeon Club, the person can use either the button Pay $308.48 or the button Change Payment Method, or use the Back button to leave this screen.

Sometimes, icons are used without words. Using an icon can also help reduce the number of words visible on screen. The Back button appears without words, but screen readers used by people with low vision or blindness will speak the availability of that button. In general, the same rules apply to these unseen words: the button will perform best if it maximizes clarity, is one or two words, and uses the same words the person would use in conversation.

Another type of button is an option in a menu or list. For these buttons, nouns are sometimes more appropriate. For example, the 'appee menu gives the player access to the images they saved, their friends, the settings for the experience, and help (Figure 4-6).

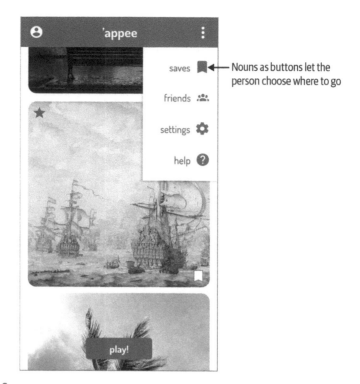

Nouns as buttons let the person choose where to go

FIGURE 4-6

The 'appee menu is the way to access the player's saves, friends, settings, and help, which are examples of noun-based buttons in a menu or list.

Each menu item can be considered as its own button, but they all need to be designed in context, the way they will be used. This way, the words can be selected to differ widely from one another so that they are easy to disambiguate. They can also be selected to make sense as a set of options, together. As 'appee shows, using only one or two words for each button enables the player to scan the options at a glance. This design consideration will make it easier for people to choose the right option, the first time, every time.

When paired with single-action titles, buttons are most effective when they match the words in the title. For example, when a person needs to create an account in TAPP, they encounter the title "Create an Account" (Figure 4-7). The button that lets the person take that action, labeled "Create Account," matches the title. Because these two phrases match so closely, there is no ambiguity: the person is committing the single action specified by the title. If the button said "Save" or "Submit," it would be less clear to the person that they were taking the intended action.

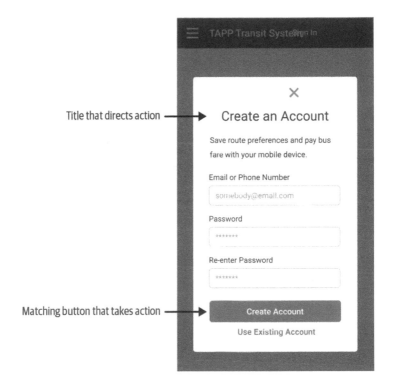

Title that directs action ⟶ Create an Account

Matching button that takes action ⟶ Create Account

FIGURE 4-7
When someone needs to create a new account in TAPP, the title "Create an Account" intentionally matches the button "Create Account." That symmetry reinforces the action to be taken.

In many cases, the button and title aren't enough by themselves. The person might need additional information to be successful. They might need a reminder of the value of taking the action, and the space in the title and button is limited. To set expectations about how the experience will behave, or just to reinforce the brand, the experience can use descriptions.

Descriptions

Purpose: Help people move forward in the experience knowing what to expect, establish the brand, and reduce liability.

A description is an informational chunk of text, sometimes called *body text*. Descriptions can appear as phrases, sentences, or paragraphs. A description can also be hidden text so that screen readers can explain a heavily visual design. Interacting with the description (tapping, clipping, hovering, etc.) has no effect. (When a description has inline links or icons to tap, consider those links or icons as following the Buttons pattern.)

Most descriptive text can meet its purposes only if people read it. Descriptions are frequently ignored. Some designers despise them as "a wall of text." People don't come to the experiences to read the UX text.

If description text is necessary, we should make it as easy to use as possible. In English, people using an interface will rapidly scan lines up to about 50 characters wide, which is enough space for about three to six words. Similarly, people's eyes will linger on a few of the words when a paragraph of text has three lines or fewer. Those few words are the description's opportunity to catch their attention long enough for understanding to develop.

When a single chunk of text becomes longer than these rough guidelines, people's eyes stop lingering on the individual words. They begin to feel more doubtful about it. Research participants and teammates will begin to remark about the "wall of text." Keeping the text brief and separating ideas into scannable chunks makes people feel more confident about their own understanding and capability to use the experience successfully.

AVOID ASTERISKS (*)

Trust is essential. We reduce trust when we give people beautiful promises and easy paths forward, but take those promises away with asterisks and fine print. When we make clarifications and disclosures difficult to read, we communicate that we're willing to work to hide things from them. Using asterisks indicates that the main text isn't fully honest, and can't be trusted.

If there are complex ideas that must be included while somebody is using the experience, include those ideas in descriptions. Use plain language, and include how it benefits the organization and the person using the experience, as necessary. This usually requires coordinating closely across the product owners, attorneys, privacy professionals, and business owners.

For example, The Sturgeon Club includes a messaging system within its experience, as shown in Figure 4-8. The Sturgeon Club uses a description at the end of the message list that sets expectations for members that the message system is secure, that it works only within the club, and that messages are deleted after 30 days. Although it can be useful information to the member, and certainly useful for The Sturgeon Club to have told them, the member doesn't need to read the text to successfully use the messaging system.

FIGURE 4-8
This Sturgeon Club Messages screen has two read and two unread message threads. The description at the bottom of the screen sets member expectations about how the messaging system works and indicates that messages will automatically be deleted after 30 days.

When a player wants to play, 'appee uses descriptive text on its "basic rules" page (Figure 4-9). The person doesn't need to read the description to be successful, unless they were planning on breaking the rules. The purpose of this descriptive text is to remind the player of the rules and to force acknowledgment of those rules before the person can play. This is a step that 'appee takes to reduce its liability for inappropriate images or claims of unfair votes or decisions.

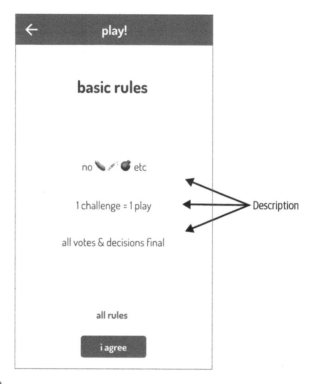

FIGURE 4-9
The basic rules screen in 'appee mostly contains descriptive text to set expectations that inappropriate sexual, drug reference, and violent topics are not allowed, that the person can play only once per challenge, and that all votes and decisions are final. This screen mostly exists to protect 'appee from claims that their rules are unavailable or unremembered.

To satisfy people who want all of the rules, who will be reassured by that wall of text, or who need specific information to continue, 'appee includes an "all rules" button. This is one way to include additional information as an option instead of as a requirement to continue.

TAPP uses descriptive text in the first screen in the "Buy Fare" process (Figure 4-10). The screen includes various passes that can be purchased by the person currently signed in, but if the person is eligible for a reduced fare, the description provides a different path forward. The rider can continue and purchase at regular price, but if they read the description, and they are eligible, they can take the steps described to get the reduced fare.

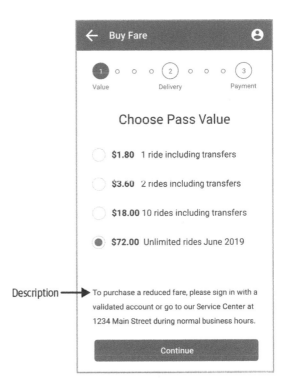

FIGURE 4-10
The first screen to buy bus fare in the TAPP experience. The description tells people that to purchase a reduced fare, they can sign in with a "validated account" or go to the physical location of the TAPP service center.

This description might feel incomplete. For example, there is no information about what a reduced fare is, or what a validated account is, or how one might know whether they qualify. To keep the text brief, scannable, and on point, that information must be optionally available. The job of this screen is to allow the rider to purchase a fare, not to become informed about the fare. The TAPP experience must provide enough information elsewhere in the experience for people to make that choice.

One of the most elegant places for titles, descriptions, and buttons to work together is in an "empty state" in the experience. When the expected action or content isn't available to the person, the experience can feel empty. Let's examine this special case of titles, descriptions, and buttons next.

Empty States

Purpose: To set expectation and build excitement while indicating that the empty space is intentional.

In my experience, teams tend to start by designing the optimal case: a person is fully engaged in the experience, using it to its best potential. When that experience is designed to highlight the things the person has already done, the same experience can feel pretty empty when the person first opens it. UX writers can use empty-state text to indicate that the emptiness is not a mistake.

Empty-state text can be as simple as a single line of text, or as complex as a title, description, and button. In the simplest case, using the format "To do X, do Y" will efficiently move people forward while emphasizing the function available (X) and the action to take (Y).

For example, when a member isn't signed in to The Sturgeon Club, no other action can be taken (Figure 4-11). The only way forward is to sign in. Even the menu is emptied to prevent people from taking any action. The empty-state text in the menu, therefore, helps members move forward: "To access your membership, sign in." The "sign in" portion is interactive text that will begin the sign-in experience.

FIGURE 4-11
When nobody is signed in to The Sturgeon Club, empty state text directs people to sign in.

In some empty-state conditions, there is nothing the person can do to fill it. In 'appee, if you open another person's profile and that other person has never submitted an image, there are no images to display. For example, the profile page for goldilox has no images to display because they've never submitted an image (Figure 4-12). The text tells the viewer "when goldilox plays, see their entries here."

when **goldilox** plays, ──────── Empty state text indicates
see their entries here   how this space could
                                      get filled

FIGURE 4-12

The view of a person's profile in 'appee usually displays the images they have entered for different challenges. When that person hasn't entered any images, other people viewing their page will understand how that space would be filled.

Empty states can get more complicated. For example, it might be impossible to give the person a one-step action to take, but they might be very interested in filling it. In TAPP, it's very handy to save a commonly used bus route. But before any bus routes are saved, the screen has no information to show (Figure 4-13).

Instead of displaying simply "No routes saved," TAPP uses the opportunity to educate the person about how to save those routes. The empty state provides the instruction "To save a route, tap Save when you find the route you want." Then, it provides a button to find a route. Together, the instructions and the action move the person toward successfully saving a route.

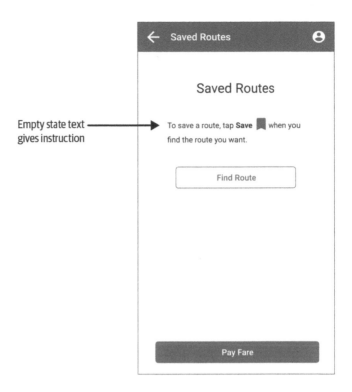

Empty state text gives instruction

FIGURE 4-13

When no routes are saved, TAPP instructs the person on how to save a route. Then, it provides them a way to take the first step in following those instructions: finding a route.

Descriptions, buttons, and titles are great tools for empty states. But when the experience is the opposite of empty—when it's full of rich detail—we need a specialized form of description: labels.

Labels

Purpose: Minimize the effort required to understand the experience.

Labels are noun phrases and adjectives that name or describe things. They are used to indicate sections, categories, status, progress, quantity, or unit. Labels are ubiquitous where there is a lot of detail to convey, because they communicate a lot of information in a compact, no-nonsense format. But even labels deserve attention: they still need to be chosen, align to voice, and be translated and/or internationalized.

The difference between a description and a label, in these text patterns, is a matter of length and purpose. Descriptions are usually full sentences, regardless of punctuation. Labels are usually single nouns or noun pairs. Descriptions are frequently used with titles, buttons, or whole experiences. Labels are usually related to passive screen elements like icons or sections and limited to that local context.

To meet their purpose, labels must use specific terms and avoid unfamiliar jargon. If vague terms are used, or jargon that the person doesn't understand, the labels can increase the effort to understand the experience. Labels are an important place to use usability testing and other user research to uncover the words a person would naturally use for these labels. The words that are already in their brain will be the easiest ones for people to read and understand.

Labels are frequently complicated by including dynamic elements. That is, the UX writer won't know what the cost of an item might be, nor the date, nor the number of "Likes" a social media post might garner. To be successful, the writer will need to know the variables they are working with and choose words that will work with all possible values of those variables.

For example, on the Folio screen of The Sturgeon Club, the labels include the date label, section labels, the monetary labels that indicate the cost of each item, and the text label "No Charge" (Figure 4-14). When this Folio experience is created, the date label could be written as: "Prepared {date}", where {date} represents the date that the folio was prepared for the club member. The format of the date needs to be further specified as the name of the month, then the number of the day, then a comma, and then the year. It's often up to the UX writer to specify that date format, in partnership with design and engineering.

Engineers should use existing code libraries, when available, for number formats like dates and money, but those labels should be checked. For The Sturgeon Club Folio, the decision had to be made to use a minus sign, instead of putting the dollar amount in parentheses. Perhaps members were asked, in a research scenario, how they would expect adjustments or payments to be indicated. The Sturgeon Club charges in US dollars exclusively, so it makes sense to use "$" and "." to separate dollars and cents, but an experience also available in Europe would need to consider how it would use "€" and "," to correctly represent the numbers.

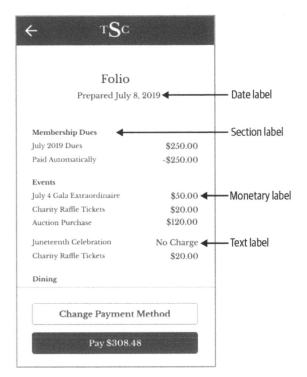

FIGURE 4-14

The Sturgeon Club Folio screen, which uses labels to indicate date, sections, currency and quantity of money, and when there is no charge.

In the 'appee experience, when a person views an image, they can also see several labels that show statistics about that image (Figure 4-15). A row of icons acts as buttons, even though no visible button text is provided. This is usable only if the icons are instantly recognizable, but it is aligned with 'appee's voice of using fewer words than strictly necessary. Instead, the labels provide context: the person can see (or hear, using a screen reader) that more than 12,000 other people have left comments, 593 people have made purchases related to this image, more than 102,000 people have "liked" the image, and more than 382,000 people have saved it. The 'appee decision to use a lowercase "k+" to indicate "more than … thousand" is another reflection of its voice to use sentence case when providing insights.

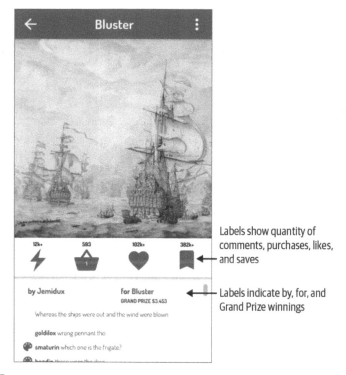

FIGURE 4-15

Labels on the 'appee view image screen indicate the quantity of comments, purchases, likes, saves, and winnings of the image and differentiate between the player and challenge.

The 'appee labels "by" and "for," which indicate the artist and challenge, respectively, are in danger of not localizing well, because not every language uses prepositions the way English does. The content creator should work with their internationalization expert and designer to create alternate layouts, in case longer words are needed to convey the same meaning in other languages. For example, the alternate label "artist" or "player" could be used instead of "by," if it could be placed vertically above the player's name.

When a rider is buying bus fare in the TAPP experience, there is space designed to include localizable progress labels (Figure 4-16). The labels indicate the name of the steps to be taken, and after the step is taken, it changes to reflect the choice made.

Labels are a specialized form of description, in that they tend to be briefer and more technical, but they are still distinct from buttons because people merely read them. Now let's go one level deeper into specialization: the unique names and statuses for controls.

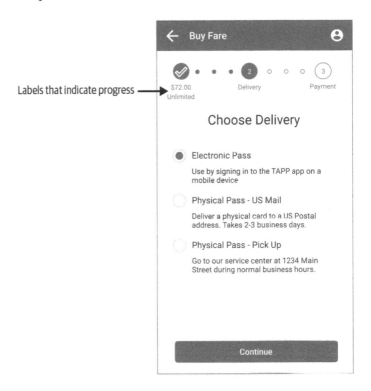

Labels that indicate progress

FIGURE 4-16
The second step of buying bus fare in the TAPP experience. The icons and labels work together to indicate which decisions have been made and which steps will be taken next.

Controls

Purpose: Inform people of the extent and state of possible customizations.

To write for controls, I find it helpful to acknowledge that any of our controls use as their core metaphor the analog dials, switches, sliders, and indicator buttons of early electronics and mechanical devices. In most meaningful ways, the use of the physical and software switches is the same. At its best, the categories and labels make the possible range of customization clear.

There are usually at least two pieces of text to consider for any particular control: name and state. The name should be the noun or verb phrase that names or describes the control in a way the person using the experience will recognize. The state of the control is, for example, whether a checkbox is checked, the position of a slider, or whether a toggle is flipped left, right, up, or down.

The UX text that is paired with the control needs to match the possible states of the control. For example, a checkbox indicates the affirmative when checked, and the negative when not checked. If we don't choose a name that has a clear meaning in the affirmative and in the negative, it won't work with its checkbox.

The setting state text can be visible or invisible, but a screen reader will still read it out loud. Checkboxes will be read as "checked" or "unchecked." Toggle switches have implied states of on or off, but might be labeled with a similarly opposite pair of states: Red/Green (with differentiation for people who are red/green colorblind), Enable/Disable, or other. Sliders and dials can use state text to establish the endpoints of the range, or use the implied text of Maximum and Minimum.

We also need to consider grouping controls together in a list. The Settings page from The Sturgeon Club demonstrates how much work a group name does to set context for the controls (Figure 4-17). Each control could be listed separately: "Show Today's Events on home screen," "Show New Messages on home screen," and so on. But grouping them together makes the whole list easier to understand, with less reading. This parallel construction makes it easier for the reader to understand not only each list item, but also how the whole set of items works together.

Toggle switches can be
On or Off

Checkboxes imply Yes if
checked, No if unchecked

FIGURE 4-17
The Sturgeon Club settings allow members to switch notifications on or off by type. They can also choose which kind of content to show on their view of the home screen.

Another consideration for the name of a control is how the person will be directed to it when they need help. For this reason, having a unique name for each control can be important, even if those controls appear in different sections of the same page. Category names can be verb phrases, like "Show on home screen" in The Sturgeon Club, and they can be noun phrases, like "Account" and "Notifications" on the TAPP settings page (Figure 4-18).

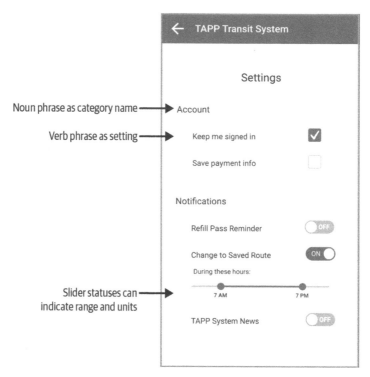

Noun phrase as category name →

Verb phrase as setting →

Slider statuses can →
indicate range and units

FIGURE 4-18

TAPP uses parallel construction at the category level, with nouns "Account" and "Notifications" setting context for those sections. The control names in the Account category are verb phrases that are related to the person's account. In Notifications, each control is named with a descriptive phrase.

The usability of the control depends on the person recognizing the purpose of the control and understanding how that matches to their own needs. Similarly, people need to recognize what kind of text to enter in text input fields, whether it's there for a message, number, password, or other kind of text. Next, we examine text field labels, hint text, and default text.

Text Input Fields

Purpose: Help people enter accurate information.

Form fields use UX text as labels, hints, and prefilled text for entering text, email addresses, numbers, dates, and other information.

The best way to help people enter accurate information is to prefill the text field with correct information. Using that information to prefill the text field will save the person time and give them the opportunity to correct it. But this works only if the experience already knows that information and knows that it is very likely to be correct.

When we can't prefill the text field, we use labels outside of the text field as well as hints within the text fields to indicate what content the person should enter.

With hint text, we need to be careful. Some research indicates that people can interpret hints as prefilled text. When we do decide to offer hint text, the label and hint can work together to provide more guidance than either one could provide separately.

For either the label or hint text, there are four good options for the text:

- Name of the information to be entered

- Example of the information to be entered

- Verb-first instructions about entering information

- Guidance for how the person can be successful

Using these options consistently can help build a person's confidence that they are entering text correctly. But even more important than consistency is clarity. If you can make the path forward clearer and make people more successful, it's better to use inconsistent options for the UX text pattern on the same screen.

For example, the Change Password overlay in The Sturgeon Club experience contains a New Password entry field (Figure 4-19). The hint provides guidance of what will work in that field: "At least 8 numbers or letters." In the same screen, the other two text fields have their own pair of label and hint designed to support the success of the member.

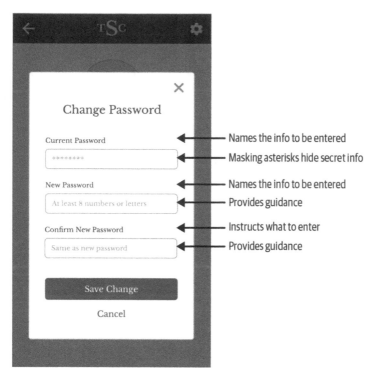

Names the info to be entered

Masking asterisks hide secret info

Names the info to be entered

Provides guidance

Instructs what to enter

Provides guidance

FIGURE 4-19

For The Sturgeon Club, when a person wants to change their password, they need to enter their current password, then their new password, and then their new password again to confirm it. The design uses pairs of labels and hints to help the member change their password successfully.

In some cases, a team might choose to use only hint text and avoid using labels. In many cases, this can help the design "look clean" and minimal. In those cases, the hint text must do all of the work of informing the person what text they should enter. When the person begins to enter information, there will be no label for the text box, so it's not a design pattern that maximizes usability.

For example, signing in to 'appee requires the person to use their phone or email address and their password (Figure 4-20). The hints are the names of the information to be entered: "email or phone" and "password." 'appee relies on the player's recognition of this common pattern to successfully sign in.

Hint names the
information to
be entered

FIGURE 4-20

The 'appee sign-in screen uses the names of the information to be entered
(email or phone along with password) in its two text fields. Note that 'appee
is making a decision that is counter to best practices for usability: when the
person begins entering information, there is no label to indicate what should
go in either input field.

The Request Help screen in the TAPP experience provides an example
for default text field entries (Figure 4-21). TAPP has an email address
for this signed-in TAPP rider, so their email address is entered for them
by default when they come to the page. The person might enter a different email address, but they don't need to.

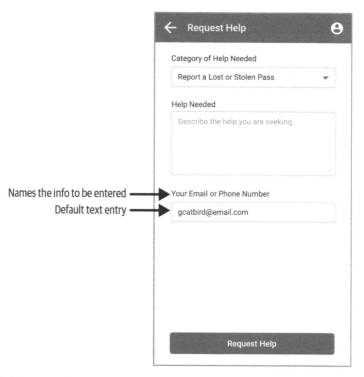

Names the info to be entered ⟶ Your Email or Phone Number

Default text entry ⟶ gcatbird@email.com

FIGURE 4-21

On the Request Help screen in TAPP, the email or phone number associated with their TAPP account appears in the text field by default.

When a person has successfully used a set of text fields, there's often a pause while the system transmits and/or validates those inputs. That pause can be stressful for the person, especially if the information they entered is sensitive, like a credit card number, or complex like an online job application, or emotionally fraught such as a message sent to a romantic interest. A kind, easy step for the experience to take is to make that pause visible. Although a spinner or other animation is usually enough for a person with full vision, we can provide text on the screen or for the screen reader to help with that transition.

Transitional Text

Purpose: Confirm that an action is happening.

When an experience "hangs," or is delayed while an action is processed, it's courteous to inform the person that their waiting is not in vain. Just as a person at a help counter will say, "Just a moment while I get that from the back," a digital experience can use transitional text to indicate that it has received a request, and the person will need to wait for a moment.

In general, transitional text shouldn't require any additional action or taps from the person. If the action is in progress, use the present continuous tense of the verb, like "is uploading" or "are sending." Ellipses help to indicate that the delay will be brief.

For example, after a person updates their payment method in The Sturgeon Club, they get an overlay message that the updating continues (Figure 4-22). They can feel confident that they have done what they intended to do, and that if they wait, the process will complete. Showing this message also prevents the club member from using the old payment method accidentally before the process is complete.

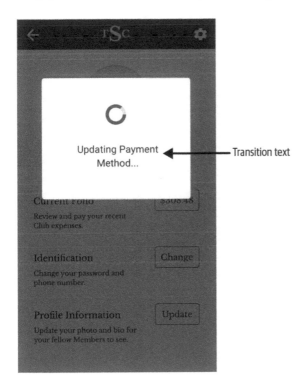

FIGURE 4-22

Transitional text in The Sturgeon Club helps build the club member's confidence that they have successfully done their part to update their payment information, while setting the expectation that the process of updating will be complete in a few moments.

If it's appropriate in the experience, a sense of excitement can be heightened by a delay. In 'appee, it can take a few moments between when a person agrees to the rules and when the current challenge is retrieved from the service. That delay can even be extended to build anticipation further to ensure that even if the database responds quickly, the player has a few moments for anticipation to build. The transitional text in Figure 4-23 emphasizes that the challenge is being prepared, and that there's "no turning back now."

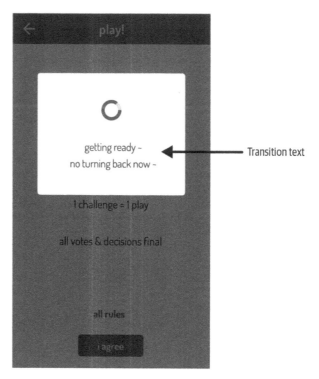

FIGURE 4-23

When a player agrees to the rules, there is a delay while 'appee retrieves the current challenge and registers this person for this challenge. The transitional text helps to build excitement with the phrase "no turning back now ~," even as it confirms that progress is happening with the more common phrase "getting ready ~."

Generic verbs like "getting" work well for many ambiguous circumstances, but in most cases, specific words work better. When a rider taps a "Map" button for a particular route, they expect a map of the route and possibly details about its closest stop. When TAPP experiences a delay in retrieving those details, it still responds to the "Map" button the person used in the transition text (Figure 4-24).

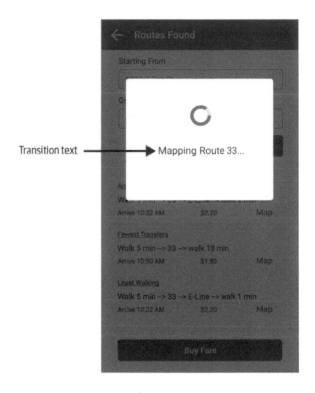

Transition text —————▶ Mapping Route 33...

FIGURE 4-24
When TAPP has a delay retrieving route map and data, it displays the transitional text "Mapping Route {number}..." to build confidence that it is working on performing the action that the person requested.

After the transitional text, the changing of the experience can be its own confirmation. In the example in Figure 4-24, when the map appears, the transition clearly is complete. But when the effect is more subtle, it's a good idea to provide a confirmation message.

Confirmation Messages

Purpose: Reassure the person that the progress or results they expect are complete.

Confirmation messages reassure the person that otherwise invisible processes are complete. These are especially useful when the result of an action is delayed. These confirmations can appear passively in the experience while the person continues forward, or they can appear in sequence in the experience as a momentary pause or step.

The basic pattern for confirmation messages is to use the past tense of the verb or verb phrase that best describes the action. In English, using one verb in the present continuous tense for transition (submitting), and the same verb with the past tense for the confirmation (submitted) can provide a sense of completion. Similar verb pairs include sending/sent, removing/removed, deleting/deleted, and posting/posted.

Confirmation messages allow the experience to continue while other systems work. For example, The Sturgeon Club provides the transitional text "Saving..." while a person is entering text, and the confirmation "Draft Saved" when a person pauses as they enter a message in the secure messaging system (Figure 4-25). Similar messages can be seen in Google Docs and Microsoft Word Online when the document is being saved online in real time.

Confirmation message appears when the person pauses in their typing

FIGURE 4-25

When someone is composing a message in The Sturgeon Club and then pauses, a message of "Draft Saved" appears to confirm that their message is saved as a draft.

The confirmation text can be a single word when the context and action to be completed is the person's sole focus. When a person submits an image to 'appee, the transition text "submitting your entry ~" is replaced by the single word "submitted!" (Figure 4-26).

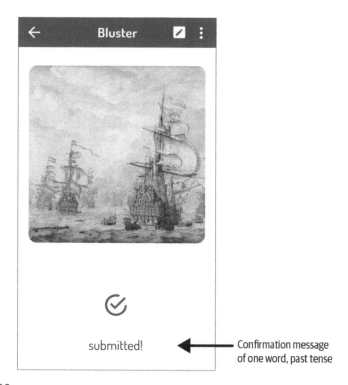

Confirmation message
of one word, past tense

FIGURE 4-26

After a player submits an entry for an 'appee challenge, "submitted!" appears to confirm the image has been safely sent to the service.

In the case of a long delay, which could be several minutes to several days, providing clarity for the person might avoid additional support or operational costs for the organization. For example, when a person sends a comment and requests a response in TAPP, there can be a delay of up to 10 business days before TAPP responds. Therefore, after the person leaves the comment, they get confirmation text of "Comment Sent" and additional information about the expected response time (Figure 4-27).

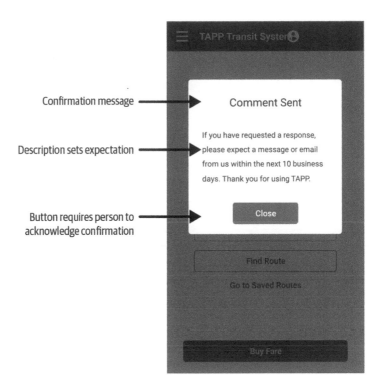

Confirmation message

Description sets expectation

Button requires person to
acknowledge confirmation

FIGURE 4-27

When a person sends a comment to TAPP, they get an immediate message
that confirms that the comment was sent and sets expectations that any
response should come within 10 business days. Adding a button to close the
dialog, instead of having it disappear after some amount of time, requires the
person to acknowledge the confirmation.

Confirmation messages are essential tools at the end of some journeys
in the experience. But when there is more that the person could be
doing or critical information they could act on, we need a special, inter-
rupting kind of message to encourage or engage a person into the experience: notifications.

Notifications

Purpose: Inform or remind a person to engage with the experience.

Notifications interrupt people to get them to pay attention to a part
of the experience that they aren't paying attention to at the moment.
They are reminders or information that should always have value and
be urgent (or at least time-appropriate) for the person receiving them.

Notifications must communicate that value and their timeliness at a glance, and include the first action the person needs to take to realize that value.

People can get notifications on the lock screen of their mobile device, in a notification center, or as a banner. Notifications can be temporary or persistent. There are different controls for these views on mobile devices, desktop and laptop computers, and in browsers and browser extensions. In general, a writer can investigate the variety of ways a notification can be displayed for their experience and should consider if and how the same text might appear in all of them.

A notification is made of at least one but frequently two pieces of text, similar to other title and description patterns. The title can usually begin with the verb that relates to the action they need to take, and convey any information necessary to create success. The description adds "nice to have" information that isn't necessary to the person's success.

For example, members of The Sturgeon Club receive a notification when there are new messages waiting for them (Figure 4-28). In the title, the person gets the instruction "View a new message" with the additional information "from a Club Member." Messages from the concierge would presumably say "View a new message from the Concierge." Because the club doesn't want to reveal the contents of the message in a notification, the description could have been omitted, but The Sturgeon Club chooses to emphasize its brand by including "Message details secured within The Sturgeon Club."

As long as the information is present, there is room for humor and even obfuscation, if it is part of the voice and entices the person to interact. For example, 'appee challenges are time-based, and are not revealed to the player until they commit to play. But 'appee can hint at the challenge to entice the player (Figure 4-29). The essential context is given by the app name that appears with any notification, so the notification is only one piece of text. Using 'appee voice, it's difficult to understand: "what's both (a lollipop) and (a rocketship) but never (candy)? new challenge! (alarm clock)."

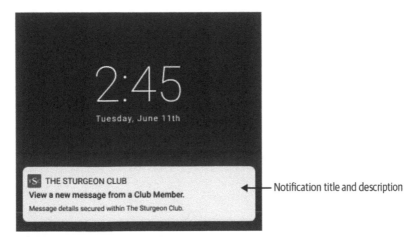

Notification title and description

FIGURE 4-28

A notification from The Sturgeon Club indicates that the person has a new message from a fellow member of the club.

Notification title and description

FIGURE 4-29

When a new challenge is available in 'appee, players receive a notification designed to pique their curiosity. In this example, emoji are used to create a riddle preceding the key information: "new challenge!"

Sometimes, notifications aren't enticing or interesting; rather, they are delivering bad news. That bad news should still have intrinsic value to the person. Because notifications are interruptions, even bad news should still be time sensitive and/or time appropriate. For example, when a person has saved a route in TAPP, they will receive notifications when that route is interrupted (Figure 4-30). In this example, the key information is the detour of a route. If the person is trying to ride that route at that moment, the description directs the person to take action: "Tap to find alternate stops."

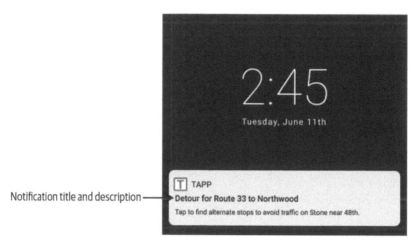

Notification title and description

FIGURE 4-30

When detours happen on a particular route, TAPP notifies riders who have saved that route. In this case, the notification indicates the bus route and direction, and that tapping the notification will provide alternate stops.

Notifications are useful to drive engagement, which is a key success metric for most digital experiences. Because it is so useful, it is easy to overuse them, which can lead to people turning off those notifications entirely. Therefore, when planning notifications, plan them as part of the entire experience. For example, the team should consider how many notifications a person could receive in a day and at what times. By providing controls to customize notifications, you enable people to limit the notifications to the ones they are actually interested in.

Many organizations reserve the use of notifications for positive interactions: getting deals in a shopping app, unlocking prizes in a game, receiving messages from friends. But that leaves out an important class of messages that are critical to the brand: errors.

Errors

Purpose: Help people get where they want to go and, if necessary, indicate that there's a problem getting there the way they intended.

Error conditions are what happens when the person can't get where they're going in the experience. Error messages are often the first way we repair the break in the virtuous cycle (Chapter 1, Figure 1-7). Our purpose is to help people move forward, and error conditions are no exception to this rule. When errors occur, text can create detours and provide maps for the person to navigate where they want to go.

Error messages are possibly the most important place in any experience to empathize with the person trying to use the experience, and to maintain the voice. To do this, the UX writer needs to stay focused on helping the person do what they were trying to do. Grammatically, this frequently means using verb-first, brief instructions, the same way titles and descriptions work when there is no error.

To maintain trust, avoid assigning blame to the person. Even if the error is their fault, blame won't help. When moving forward isn't possible, make that clear. If an apology is appropriate in the conversation and in the brand, apologize for the delay, loss, inconvenience, or disappointment to the person.

For an experience that people depend on for work—like most people who work in offices, engineers, designers, writers, IT professionals, and more—additional details about the error condition can help. Beyond satisfying their sense of curiosity, we need to satisfy their sense of responsibility. They want to make sure they didn't do anything wrong and that there is nothing more they could or should do. Giving them more detail will help give them a sense of the circumstances they could use to identify or predict the error in the future.

For general audiences, sometimes called "consumer" audiences, add details or links to more information from errors only if those details will help the person move forward or feel more confident or reassured about the experience, their data, or your organization. Note that everybody, in some aspect of their life, is a member of the general audience—even engineers, designers, and IT pros. The example experiences in this book anticipate general audiences, so these error text patterns do not include professional-level details.

There are three main categories of errors in software experiences, organized by how much they interrupt the person:

- Inline error

- Detour error

- Blocking error

The least intrusive interruption is an inline error, where the person is advised to make a correction before they can move forward. The text can be very short and, in general, can clarify, remind, or instruct an ongoing conversation between the person and the experience instead of stopping their actions.

For example, if someone enters something that isn't a 10-digit number when signing in to The Sturgeon Club, they receive an error message that instructs them to enter a 10-digit phone number (Figure 4-31). This way, the club can avoid telling the member they did something wrong. They can also satisfy the member's intent more rapidly if they just instruct them on how to do the right thing.

In cases like these for which the experience is working to validate the contents of the field before continuing, it might seem natural to the engineering team to call any incorrect contents "invalid." That entry has, after all, failed validation. But most organizations will prefer to avoid such emotionally laden words: people rarely want to be told that they have failed, and it's rarely the best way to encourage them to move forward. Also consider that "invalid" has been used in the United States to describe people with disabilities and is viewed as an ableist word. When we're working with words, we are always working with the history of those words. It's worth the work to provide a positive way forward instead of making people feel bad.

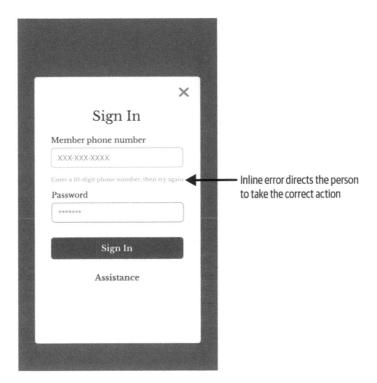

Inline error directs the person
to take the correct action

FIGURE 4-31

When signing in to The Sturgeon Club, if a person doesn't enter a 10-digit number in the phone number field, they receive instruction about what to enter.

When an experience can't be corrected inline, we can hang a virtual "detour" or "out of order" sign using error messages. These errors occur when the person can't get where they want to go in the way they anticipated, but they can still get there.

Detour messages should have the main instruction in the most prominent spot. For a real-life example, when there is construction on a road, the DETOUR signs should be more prominent than the explanation for the detour. In 'appee, when a payment method is declined, the error message provides instruction first, then explanation, and then the single action to take to move forward (Figure 4-32). Following the title and button patterns described earlier, the button matches the words in the title; even if the description is never read, the person can continue and be successful.

Sometimes, the way forward is blocked until the person takes an action that is outside of the scope of the experience. Whether the error is an outage (planned or unplanned) for the entire experience or a missing web address (404 error), make it clear that they've reached the end of the road. If possible, specify when or under what conditions the experience will be available again.

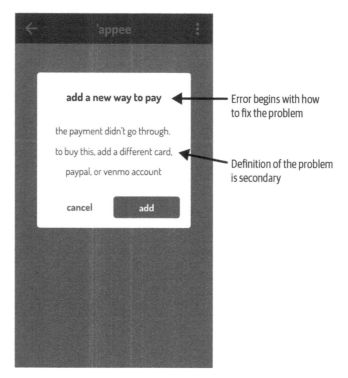

FIGURE 4-32

For whatever reason a payment is declined, 'appee presents a way forward: add a new way to pay. By focusing on the solution, 'appee stays out of the person's relationship with their financial institution, and helps them complete the task that both the person and 'appee are most interested in.

For example, an experience that relies on an internet connection can't govern that connection any more than a vending machine can fix bubblegum in its coin slot. In Figure 4-33, the device needs to connect to the internet before a person can use TAPP to buy bus fare or find a route. Therefore, the error is unambiguous, starting with the title, "Connect to the Internet."

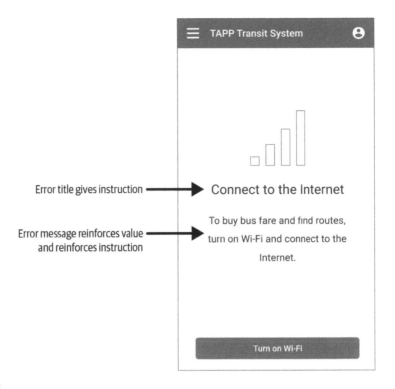

FIGURE 4-33

When WiFi is turned off, TAPP provides an error message that begins with why they might want to connect and then instructs them on what they will need to do to proceed.

Then, TAPP reinforces the value it could be providing—buying bus fare and finding routes—and repeats what the person needs to do: connect to the internet. This pattern of instruction in the title, then the value, then a repetition of the instruction can support people who are tentative users of the experience.

Summary: Use Patterns as a Place to Start

The UX text patterns in this chapter are supported by the proprietary research I conducted and consumed at Microsoft, Google, and OfferUp while creating experiences for people to use at work and at play.

All of these patterns are models, so like any model, they will be wrong in some circumstances. Just because these patterns have worked for millions of people doesn't mean that they are the best options in all circumstances. Instead, I hope they provide a guideline to draft usable text. Then, you can edit that text into the best possible options for your experience.

[5]

Edit, Because They Didn't Go There to Read

I try to leave out the parts that people skip.
—ELMORE LEONARD, WRITER

EDITING IS THE PROCESS of iterating the text to make sure that it meets its purpose, it's concise, it's conversational, and it's clear to the person using the experience.

Although spelling and punctuation are important, we are not limited to these basics. Instead, by imagining even radical changes to the text, we can edit our way to achieving the goals of the organization, the brand, and the people who will use the experience.

It is essential to edit text inside the designs, seeing the text in place on the screen as you edit. The text will be read and be understood differently if it is moved in the apparent hierarchy of a screen or even if it wraps differently. By working in the design, we can vary which words have prominence and keep our eyes on width and length, and leave enough space for translated UX text to grow longer. More information about the tools and process of editing text in the design is in Chapter 7.

Editing can be a fluid process in which many variables are changed as inspiration strikes. But this isn't a book about how to make inspiration strike, so in this chapter, I present the structured process that works for me—even when inspiration is taking a break.

Editing in Four Phases

We want the text to meet at least these four goals:

- Purposeful

- Concise

- Conversational

- Clear

It is possible to tackle all of them at once, but to illustrate a repeatable process, let's go through them in phases. When we start, we have a first draft or current state of the text. Then, we make sure the text meets all of its purposes. In this phase, the UX text can grow far too long— but don't panic: as editing progresses, the text will become shorter and work harder (Figure 5-1).

Next, we work on making the text concise. After it's short, we adjust it until it is conversational again, not sterile or robotic. Finally, we check to ensure that the meaning will be clear to the person using the experience.

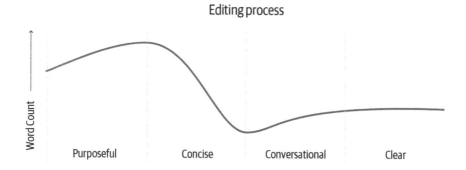

FIGURE 5-1

The editing process curve illustrates how word length tends to increase from the draft state through the purposeful phase and then drops in the concise phase before rising slowly through the conversational and clear phases.

Purposeful

As an example, we look at a notification TAPP sends to people who renew their passes automatically when their credit card has expired. The original text for this notification has a title and description: "Payment Method Expiring: Monthly Pass Will Not Be Renewed" (Figure 5-2). The notification doesn't tell the person what they need to do to fix the problem and isn't in TAPP voice.

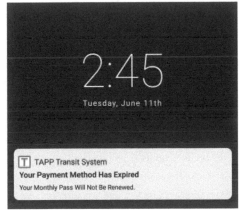

This notification doesn't tell the person how to move forward, and isn't in TAPP voice.

FIGURE 5-2

The original text for the notification seen by TAPP riders if the payment method they use for a recurring, automatic purchase of a monthly pass is expiring.

We begin by making sure that the UX text will meet its purpose for the person and for the organization. To understand the person's purpose, we need to imagine what that experience is like for them. Because they buy a monthly bus pass automatically, we can probably assume that they're a regular bus rider. Imagine if they usually get on the bus and scan their pass without thinking about it—after all, they have set it up to not have to think about it. But their credit card expired, so their bus pass wasn't renewed, so they won't be able to pay. They could be stranded without their bus pass, embarrassed by an expiration date that they didn't even notice. Yikes!

If this is true, we can probably assume that they are interested in updating their payment method. Our notification can help with that.

We also need to imagine the purpose for the TAPP organization and the potential impact of the message. One of the main purposes of the experience is to collect bus fare in a way that's convenient for the rider and for the transit system. But TAPP's larger purpose is to provide transit for its community. An essential part of meeting that larger purpose is to foster goodwill toward transit in general, and to make transit seem like an easy, convenient option. TAPP can assume its relationship with this regular rider is adequate, but it needs to strive for more than adequacy: TAPP's regular riders are the most likely champions for transit.

So now we know the purposes this notification needs to meet:

- Pay fare without embarrassment

- Update the payment method

- Reinforce positive relationship

We also have the TAPP voice chart (Chapter 2, Table 2-22), which reminds us to consider including these concepts: waste no resource, every ride on time, and rides for every rider. It's possible that none of these will be great to include this time, but we can keep an eye on it.

With those purposes and concepts in mind, we can create a few new versions of our original message (Figure 5-3).

Not every option includes every purpose, and that's OK. The job of this notification is to get people into the process for updating their payment method. To measure success of this notification, the team can compare expiration date update rate before and after the notification is released, among people who have automatic payments. The additional purposes have longer-term effects on brand affinity and recognition.

Before we release this notification, though, we have more editing work to do. The notification is bulked up with all of those purposes and seems awfully long. It's so long, in fact, that a couple of them are difficult to understand. The purpose of the notification is no longer clear. Our next step will take the best of the examples, and work to make it concise.

Purposes to satisfy:
- Pay fare without embarrassment
- Update the payment method
- Reinforce positive relationship

Voice concepts:
- Waste no resource
- Every ride on time
- Rides for every rider

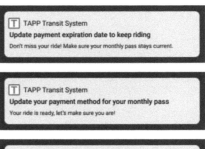

FIGURE 5-3

Four options for the TAPP notification to inform a regular rider that the payment method used to purchase their monthly pass has expired, based on addressing as many of the purposes for the notification as possible.

Concise

There are two great reasons to reduce the amount of text in an experience. The first is that nobody came to the experience to read the UX text (except us UX writers, but we're not the main audience). The other is the limit of usable space for text in the experience.

People find it easiest to scan text when it is 40 or fewer characters wide, and three or fewer lines long. But when writing for an experience that will be localized in several languages, we should use only half to two-thirds of the space for English text because several languages tend to take up more space.

When we don't plan enough space, design elements can run over one another or off of the screens. Conversely, when we don't use space wisely, character-based languages can leave distracting, unplanned blank spaces. Especially for description text, it's important to work with design and development partners to create forgiving designs that flow to longer and shorter text as appropriate for the language.

Editing for concision is a process of winnowing down phrases to their core meanings. Then, we try out different sequences to find the ones that are briefest and easiest to understand.

For example, the title of the notification we'll move forward with is "To keep paying by pass, update your payment method." We can play with several different ways to start:

- Start with the imperative verb: Update your payment info to buy monthly pass

- Start with the purpose the person might recognize: To buy your monthly pass, update your payment info

- Start with the context: Monthly pass: Payment info update needed

- Start with an emotional motivator: Alert: Monthly pass payment problem

We also need to consider which idea is the most important. When three or more ideas must appear in the same sentence, it tends to be the last word or idea that will be the most powerfully remembered. Part of that is how our brains work: the most recent thing has more significance in our memory and on our actions than it otherwise would.

The first idea in a sentence is the second most powerful, because it doesn't get the power of being left at the end of the sentence. But it is scanned first, and possibly most frequently. When there is a word that will signal to the reader that they have found the idea they are seeking, that word should be the most prominent.

For our notification example, Figure 5-4 shows one of the versions created during the purpose phase as well as four iterations of editing for concision. We can write these edits sequentially, making a copy of the previous version and then removing or reordering words. We make another copy and remove and reorder words again. As we focus on being concise, the text becomes shorter and shorter.

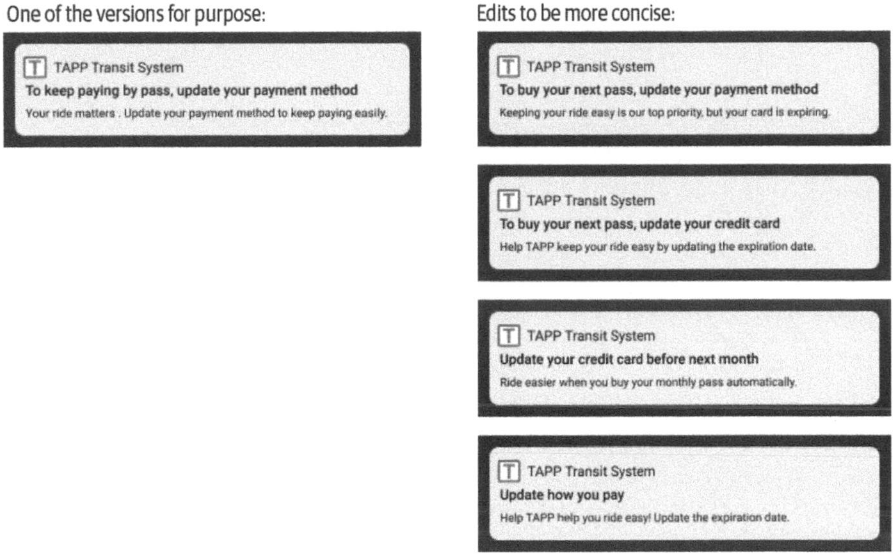

One of the versions for purpose:

```
[T] TAPP Transit System
To keep paying by pass, update your payment method
Your ride matters . Update your payment method to keep paying easily.
```

Edits to be more concise:

```
[T] TAPP Transit System
To buy your next pass, update your payment method
Keeping your ride easy is our top priority, but your card is expiring.
```

```
[T] TAPP Transit System
To buy your next pass, update your credit card
Help TAPP keep your ride easy by updating the expiration date.
```

```
[T] TAPP Transit System
Update your credit card before next month
Ride easier when you buy your monthly pass automatically.
```

```
[T] TAPP Transit System
Update how you pay
Help TAPP help you ride easy! Update the expiration date.
```

FIGURE 5-4

From one of the versions of a TAPP notification, I created four more options by editing each one to be more concise than the last.

When I'm done with this phase, I've usually edited the message down to a cryptic shell of its former self. "Update how you pay" is very brief and positive; it focuses on the action that needs to be taken but leaves out too much of the context. To keep the message clear, we don't need to continue with the shortest, most concise option. We'll use the longer "Update your credit card before next month" instead as we edit to make the text conversational.

Conversational

When we're making the UX text conversational, we might still be making radical changes to the text. We'll still be adding and removing words and changing their order, this time focusing on making the most conversational choices for the experience.

Recall from Chapter 3 that *conversational*, as we're using it here, doesn't specify a voice or tone. Instead, it means that humans can recognize they are interacting with the words; they are in conversation with the experience. It means that the text must not be so abrupt as to make it difficult to interact.

As you can see in Figure 5-5, this is the phase in which we begin to narrow down to only a few more ways to say the same thing.

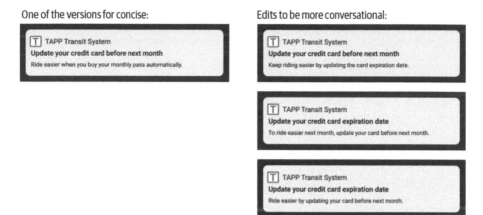

One of the versions for concise:

Edits to be more conversational:

FIGURE 5-5
From of the versions of a TAPP notification, three more options were created to be more conversational than the last.

Now that we have several options, the best editing tool is the human voice. Read the titles and descriptions as if the experience is "talking" to the person, and read the buttons, options, links, and other input fields as the person responding back to the experience. When more than one phrase will appear on the same surface, read them out loud together. For example, when there is a screen title, then a heading, and then text, read them together.

This is a great time to think about the text that screen readers will say, which includes this text and also text that won't be seen. For example, text that appears on a button might be read "Button: Pay Fare" for the button text "Pay Fare."

The words in the buttons, links, and other input options should feel like appropriate responses from the person to the experience. The words in titles, descriptions, and headings should feel like appropriate statements from the experience to the person. They also shouldn't be embarrassing, even if they were spoken by the head of the organization on a worldwide stage or printed in the *New York Times*.

Clear

Before we finish, we need to check the text for clarity. This is a great time to remind ourselves of the purpose, to reimagine where the person is, what they're doing, and why they're seeing this UX text. For complex screens and user flows, this is also a great time to check the text with teammates and to partner with user researchers to get feedback from people who will use the experience.

For clarity, the right words will be the ones that the people using the experience will recognize immediately, without having to think. In general, the more specialized the experience, the more it will need specialized terminology. But outside of their specialty, even nuclear physicists are "normal people" who use everyday words in their everyday lives. Simple, common words are more recognizable, even to specialists.

Common words often include idioms or metaphors. They litter our natural language (notice what I did there?), so it's not unusual to get to the best options and discover that only a person who speaks that language fluently would understand it. Sometimes, idioms are the best option in one language and culture but are untranslatable or offensive in others.

When proposing a text solution that uses idiom or metaphor, create a plainer alternative to be translated to other languages. Depending on the localization system, the plain alternative can be included as a "language 0" option in the code or entered into code comments.

Idiomatic translation can also can work the other direction: when a translator says, "The way we'd say this in my language is '*this metaphor*,'" believe them! Use the plain alternative in the language of development, and use that metaphor in their language.

At this point with our example notification from TAPP, we need to narrow down the best options to propose to the team. I try to propose several good options for any UX text. In the best case, I can test those options against one another to learn which text is most effective. In the worst case, I have at least demonstrated to my team that we can use the text as a versatile tool.

For the team, I write up the best options in the order I think will be most effective, and I describe the details that make them different from each other (Figure 5-6). Note that these options didn't all come from the end of the process; sometimes, a gem comes out of the very early edits. It's difficult to admit that more work doesn't always make creative output better, but we'd be silly not to use our best work.

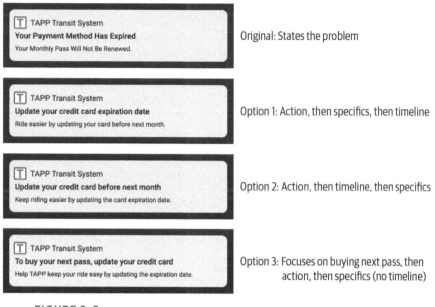

T TAPP Transit System **Your Payment Method Has Expired** Your Monthly Pass Will Not Be Renewed.	Original: States the problem
T TAPP Transit System **Update your credit card expiration date** Ride easier by updating your card before next month.	Option 1: Action, then specifics, then timeline
T TAPP Transit System **Update your credit card before next month** Keep riding easier by updating the card expiration date.	Option 2: Action, then timeline, then specifics
T TAPP Transit System **To buy your next pass, update your credit card** Help TAPP keep your ride easy by updating the expiration date.	Option 3: Focuses on buying next pass, then action, then specifics (no timeline)

FIGURE 5-6

The list of final text options I share with the team. I include descriptions of the details that make each option different and list the options in the order I prefer.

If more edits are needed, I'll use the best option to create a content review document as outlined in Chapter 7, in the section "Managing Content Review" on page 142.

Summary: Use UX Text to Help People Move Forward

Wherever the original words came from, editing will help the UX text move people toward their goal, establish a positive brand association, protect the organization from liability, and disappear from the person's memory—all without making them feel like they were reading. How to measure those effects is the subject of the next chapter.

[6]

Measuring UX Content Effectiveness

If you can't measure it, you can't improve it.
—PETER DRUCKER, BUSINESS CONSULTANT

WHEN I FIND AN existing screen with UX text that is too complex, too long, or too repetitive, I bring my proposed changes to the product owner.

> "How do we know this is worth the effort?" they ask. The product owner is protecting the team's engineering time and localization cost. To make demands of those resources, I need to make the right argument.
>
> "How are you measuring success?" I ask.
>
> I listen to the explanation of their metric—or their excuse for not having a metric.
>
> The metric is usually a very specific version of "we need more people to do this thing." Sometimes, that thing is to start doing it, or finish doing it, or to become aware of it. So, I explain where the current UX text slows down the person and frustrates them from continuing. I show them how the changes I propose would make improvements.
>
> I say, "I'm confident these changes would improve your metric."

This scene was abstracted from more than a hundred conversations in at least five teams I've worked with. We reach agreement in principle and then we find when and where in the development schedule to add this work item. I offer to open a work item for engineering, both to be helpful and to keep a record of the task.

The role of the UX writer is to improve the experience by optimizing the UX content. By measuring the improvement UX writing makes in the outcomes we measure, we can demonstrate the value of investing in UX writing.

But the value is more than how many dollars the UX content can earn or save. By measuring what works and what doesn't work, we learn more about what UX content will work for these people, in this experience.

Measurements of the experience as a whole, like the number of Daily Active Users (DAU), don't give us the whole picture. For example, DAU can't distinguish between a person who stops using an experience because they don't like it and a person who stops using it because it's no longer what they need. UX research methods like interviews and surveys help us understand more about why people behave the way they do in our experiences.

Even without direct measurement, and even without new research with people using the experience, UX writers can use the wealth of usability research that already exists. Usability principles that apply to visual and interaction design already include considerations for the UX content. We can also use the voice we define to measure the UX content. By measuring against these heuristics, we can establish a baseline from which to make improvements.

In this chapter, we examine several direct measures of a person's behavior in the experience. We take a brief journey through UX research methods that help UX writers understand why people behave the way they do, that elicit people's comments, feedback, questions, and the words they're likely to understand. Finally, we examine how to use heuristics for voice and usability to "score" the UX content.

Direct Measurement of UX Content

Organizations have many ways to measure their success. How they relate those measurements to the experiences they build varies widely. For the most part, that relationship is beyond the scope of this book, but we use 'appee as an example.

'appee makes money in three ways:

- Displaying advertisements to people as they browse images
- Selling to other businesses the results of machine learning from the images uploaded and people's reactions to those images
- Selling physical items with people's uploaded images on them

To make money, therefore, 'appee wants to optimize these key behaviors:

Playing the game (and therefore uploading images)
> Without people playing, physical items can't be sold, there are no images to browse, and there aren't enough images for machine learning to be effective. Uploading images supports all three ways 'appee makes money.

Browsing images (and therefore encountering ads)
> Without people browsing, 'appee can't receive payment from ad networks for displaying the ads.

Reacting to images, including liking, blocking, and commenting
> Because people respond to images, 'appee machine learning can make the data it sells to other companies more valuable.

Buying physical items with uploaded images
> This is the lowest-margin activity because it incurs more operational cost for 'appee.

Without people engaging in these behaviors, 'appee will fail as a business. Therefore, it needs to ensure that the experience is usable, engaging, and attractive to players—and more attractive than any competitors that arise.

When 'appee measures these behaviors and then makes changes to the UX, it can learn whether the changes in the UX affect those behaviors. The best way to understand the effect of UX changes to existing experiences is to use *A/B testing*.

In A/B testing, proposed changes are released to a sample of the people using the experience (group A) to test whether they perform more of the desired behavior. A second sample is chosen as a control group (in this example, group B). When the test is set up, and the changes are ready in the experience, the changes are rolled out to group A, but not shown to group B. If version A has a meaningful effect on behavior that's better than version B, the whole experience can be changed to move everybody to version A.

Samples A and B must be chosen to make sure they are similar enough, and large enough, so that the results will have statistical significance. The test design needs to include these sampling criteria as well as the length of time the test will run, the behaviors that will be measured, and the minimum difference in behaviors between the test groups that is necessary to show meaning.

A practical consideration for A/B testing is that it isn't always possible or desirable. The experience needs to be designed with the ability to deploy different versions to different people and to measure those groups separately. It can take significant time to run the test and extract meaningful results. Early in the adoption of a new experience (or even a new feature in an experience), there just might not be enough people using it to show a difference in A/B testing.

When A/B testing is both possible and desirable, there are common behaviors that can be measured as signals for A/B testing. In this section, we consider six ways to measure the experience:

- Onboarding

- Engagement

- Completion

- Retention

- Referrals

- Cost

ONBOARDING

The onboarding pace is how long it takes, on average, for a person new to the experience to perform each of the key behaviors. To measure those lengths of time, 'appee can record the time and date for the following acts:

- A person first provides email, phone, or password

- First scroll down the main screen

- First like, comment, block, and upload

- First time the person buys an item

From these signals, 'appee can calculate how much time it usually takes for a new person to begin behaving in ways 'appee cares about. This is the baseline onboarding pace for each behavior, a concrete indicator of how quickly a new player can provide value to 'appee, and 'appee provide value to that person. The information the experience gives that person in their first few seconds in the app can have a big effect on these behaviors. The team can A/B test options for that UX text in the first-run experience, measuring the onboarding pace.

ENGAGEMENT

Engagement measures how many people are active in the experience in a particular time frame. The key for this is to define what "active" means in a way that is valuable to the organization. For many ad-supported experiences, activity can be measured as "opens the app." This activity is frequently reported as Daily Active Users (DAU) and Monthly Active Users (MAU) of the entire experience.

'appee should be engineered so that the business receives signals from the experience about what the person is doing: buying, browsing, uploading, or reacting to images. This is a measure of the viability of key behaviors to indicate that people keep coming back to the experience. Let's imagine 'appee measures active to be "starts the app and browses more than three images," and reports DAU of 1.2 million people.

When the team updates the UX content, the updates can be A/B tested to ensure that they have a positive (or at least neutral) effect on engagement. For example, there's a persistent myth I've heard among software builders that "more words mean less engagement." If more UX text is designed, we can A/B test those updates to make sure that engagement isn't reduced. Conversely, I expect they'll find that the right changes to UX content improves engagement, whether that's the UX text, the content the person consumes in the experience (for 'appee, the game themes and uploaded images), or the quality of the how-to content.

COMPLETION

Completion is when people not only engage, but also complete the key behavior. For some key behaviors, completion is the same as engagement: there is no separate "completion" of browsing, liking, or saving an image, for example. But when a person starts a more complex process like leaving a comment but then cancels, that's a case of engaging without completing.

Another way to think about completion is its opposite: abandonment. If people in 'appee start to buy an item but then abandon their shopping cart, 'appee isn't maximizing its opportunity. Similarly, if they start to upload an image but then cancel without posting it, 'appee has missed the chance to learn from that image.

When changes are made to the experience that increase completion, the experience has improved the business outcomes. When the change to the experience is a change to the UX text, it's the UX text change that improved the business outcome.

RETENTION

If engagement can be summarized as "people per day," retention can be summarized as "days per person." Most organizations making experiences, including 'appee, want people to come back to those experiences over and over again. Whether this is measured as "how many times does the average player come to 'appee each day" or "how many consecutive days does a person use 'appee," retention can be an indicator of abiding interest in the experience. Retention is often about how the experience makes the person feel, which provides an indicator of brand affinity.

When changes are made to the UX text throughout the experience, subtle effects on usability and voice can add up to surprising effects in retention. In part, this is because when the UX text reflects the voice, it can be used as a differentiator from the experience's competitors and improve retention. The event of the change itself can be used to drive awareness and marketing: blog posts and articles can highlight the experience's focus on the people who use it.

Beyond voice changes, if people find the experience difficult to use, they use it only as long as they must. When we change UX content to increase usability and people begin to prefer it over their other options, we will measure an effect on retention.

REFERRALS

Referrals happen when people who use the experience recommend it to more people. In 'appee, a person could make an indirect referral by sharing an image from the app to Facebook or Twitter. 'appee can also provide opportunities for direct referral with "Invite a friend" promotions, badges, and other opportunities to grow the number of people who come to the experience and engage in the key behaviors.

When an update to the UX content affects the functionality, usability, or brand, people can be newly reminded of friends or family who might like the experience. Of course, you should watch the referral rate especially when changes are made that directly remind people about those friends and family, and provide them new ways to connect.

REDUCING COSTS

Aside from all of these measurements related to increasing the organization's positive metrics, there are also real costs of doing business to be minimized. For example, 'appee has support costs associated with shipping items decorated with images, helping people use the experience, and moderating comments, images, and descriptions that don't follow its rules. When changes in the experience can increase understanding, discourage rule-breakers, and reduce the number of shipping mistakes, the organization can reduce costs.

But beyond A/B testing, building and updating the experience also has associated costs: hours of development, design, and decision making, for which people are paid. When efficiencies are adopted that help the team design, develop, and decide faster or even just with higher confidence, the organization saves time and energy that it can spend on more good ideas. By adopting frameworks that help the team decide on better UX content the first time and pay for its localization only once, the organization saves time and money. While they might not spend less cash overall, the organization might develop more with what they have.

Even more, A/B testing can't tell you *why* a particular piece of text is more or less effective than another. UX writers need to be able to predict whether text will be good even before direct measurement is possible, by consuming and conducting UX research and applying heuristics to help predict the effect of experience design.

Researching UX Content

UX writers need to know their audience: the people who have used, might use, or do use the experience. We need to know why people are there, what they want to do, how they think about what they're doing, and what success means for them. Conducting UX research gives us an opportunity to draw influence from people who bring experiences different from anybody else on the team.

During UX research, the UX writer needs to pay special attention to the words people actually use. The words they use to describe their intent as well as to name pieces of the experience are the words that are already in that person's head. These are the words that the person will need to spend the least effort to recognize, the words that people will scan without feeling like they are reading.

The research methods that are often useful for the UX content include the following:

- Analysis of reviews, questions, and comments
- 1:1 and small group interviews
- Codesigning exercises, like card sorting
- Usability testing
- Surveys

Hopefully, your UX team includes a UX researcher, who is conducting and helping the team conduct this kind of research. But even if there is no dedicated research resource, it's possible to benefit from doing the research that you can.

REVIEWS, QUESTIONS, AND COMMENTS

One of the easiest places to start research is in the feedback people are already providing, whether that's in app store reviews, in questions to the support team, or from a formal beta program. For example, the 'appee team can learn from the reviews and stars that players give it, mentions of it in social media, and comments made on press releases and social media.

In those comments, pay attention to where people are enthusiastic: these are the ideas, functions, and words that are resonating with people. This is where the experience has strengths to build on. Next, gather and sort the comments, reviews, or questions that don't ask for a new feature but indicate confusion or frustration about what the person can do or how they can do it. When there is this kind of usability problem, there's probably an opportunity to help the person by adjusting the UX content. Finally, where there is evidence of brand disappointment, look for opportunities to improve the voice and to set better expectations.

INTERVIEWING

Beyond your analysis of existing feedback, the most basic proactive research is to talk to the people the experience is for. You can find people by posting an ad online, putting up a sign at a library, or striking up conversations at your local mall. What's important is that you find people who genuinely represent the people your organization needs to attract.

For an organization like 'appee, reaching out to people using Instagram or putting up a sign on an artist supply shop's bulletin board could create the first few conversations. TAPP might put signs at its physical bus stops, community centers, libraries, and inside the buses. The Sturgeon Club could put a subtle message at its front desk to ask members to share their opinions.

Recruit research participants to represent viewpoints that the team knows it lacks. For example, 'appee wants to ensure that it is attractive not only to the same age group as its 24- to 38-year-old development staff, but also to teens and established, older artists. As another example, The Sturgeon Club needs to make sure that its members who aren't comfortable using mobile devices and computers are served and included. TAPP needs to ensure that adopting a new online payment system doesn't exclude people who don't have access to mobile data, who have low mobility or vision, or who might not have access to traditional banking.

When recruiting, it's important to respect your organization's disclosure policies, which might include having the person sign a non-disclosure agreement (NDA). I recommend working with a professional researcher (or even research recruiter) to design and recruit a sample set that genuinely represents the people you want to use your experience.

After you have recruited people, you can conduct interviews to learn more about them and their relationship to the experience. Start by establishing rapport with them and setting the context about what the organization is trying to do. Listen to how the people talk, and the words that they say: these are the writer's gold mine. You will be designing the conversation the experience will be having with the person, so you're seeking the words that make sense to them. They will also express excitement about the parts that are most valuable to them, and fear or disappointment about the things that worry them. By listening, you can learn about what that person wants, needs, or would like in the experience.

A specialized version of interviewing is usability testing: asking people to move through a designed experience, paying attention to their behavior and reactions to the experience, and talking with them about it. Usability testing is a rich topic, separate from its usefulness to inform UX content, which is mostly beyond the scope of this book. For the UX writer, usability testing is a specific interview type in which we get direct feedback about the designed UX content while continuing to absorb and process the language the person uses in that context.

There is a science and an art to conducting interviews without introducing bias. UX research is a rich discipline! This is a great place to partner with a researcher on your team and to consult resources for UX research. By paying attention in these interviews, the writer can design a conversation that uses the words the interviewees use, that they will find valuable, and that will also address and allay their fears. UX text informed by research will increase the value of the experience for the organization by making it more attractive and engaging, and also reduce support costs.

CODESIGNING

A step beyond interviewing is to invite people to codesign the experience. Codesigning, or designing with people, means that you are giving their purposes and concerns a voice in how the experience is designed and developed. Having these people represent themselves makes it easier to keep the experience focused on the people who will use it. Even more important, people will bring opinions and concerns about the experience that the team might not yet have considered.

The conversation design exercise described in Chapter 3 is a codesigning activity. Another activity is a card-sort exercise, in which the UX writer prepares a set of cards with words relevant to the experience beforehand. During the codesign activity, people sort the cards into groups, or sequence, or hierarchy. Another codesign activity is a "magic wand" exercise, in which people are asked, "If you had a magic wand, how would you use it to change this experience?"

SURVEYING

Interviewing 100 people might cost too much and take too much time, but asking 100 people survey questions is much more possible. When people respond to surveys, especially to free-response questions, they provide the UX writer information about the words they already associate with particular ideas—the words already in their heads.

Another use for surveys is to learn more about the effect of the text on people's perception of the experience and the brand. In these questions, we might ask people to describe the organization and the organization's competitors. You can compare the words and phrases that they use with the voice concepts that support the organization's product principles and concepts. The closer they match, the more successful the experience is at conveying those principles.

Sometimes, the team wants to learn more but doesn't have time for interviews, codesigning, and surveys. The fastest and least expensive way to analyze the UX content is to apply *heuristic analysis*: measure the UX content against rules for usability and voice, make improvements, and then measure again.

UX Content Heuristics

When it's not clear where to begin making improvements in the UX content, we can apply general rules about what makes the text in an experience "good." These general rules, called *heuristics*, can be applied by any native speaker of the language in which the text is written, when they know the organizational purpose for the experience, the purpose for the people using it, and an understanding of the organization's voice.

For this book, I've organized these heuristics into a generic scorecard that highlights how UX content can be improved. These heuristics draw from my own work and research at Xbox and OfferUp, and in part on *Nielsen Norman Group's 10 Heuristics for User Interface Design* (*https://www.nngroup.com/articles/ten-usability-heuristics*). Keeping this generic scorecard as a document template means that you can reuse and modify it for different experiences.

To use the scorecard, choose a piece of the whole experience that a person would understand as a complete task—for example, finding a route in TAPP, sending a message in The Sturgeon Club, or starting 'appee for the first time. We'll first record the goals of the person using it as well as the goals that the organization is trying to meet by providing that part of the experience. Then, we'll use each criterion in the scorecard as a 10-point scale. That is, if an experience fully meets that criterion, it gets 10 points. If it meets the criterion only a tiny bit, it might get 2 points out of 10. If a criterion doesn't apply, it is left out of the final calculation.

There is subjectivity in scoring, just like there is subjectivity in grading an essay or judging a dog breed. If we keep in mind that the points are not an absolute evaluation of an experience, we can avoid the moral overtones of "good" or "bad" UX. Instead, we will use any of these measuring techniques to focus on finding which parts of an experience to improve. Using the scorecard before making changes, and then using it again to measure suggested changes, can help the team estimate the impact they think the changes will make.

The scorecard has two main categories: Usability and Voice, with criteria in groups of Accessible, Purposeful, Concise, Conversational, and Clear. Voice has the six criteria defined by the voice chart in Chapter 2: Concepts, Vocabulary, Verbosity, Grammar, Punctuation, and Capitalization (Table 6-1).

TABLE 6-1. A blank template for scoring UX content for usability and voice

UX CONTENT SCORECARD FOR:	
Person's goals	
Organization's goals	

USABILITY			
CRITERIA		**COMMENTS**	**SCORE (0–10)**
Accessible	Available in the languages the people using it are proficient in		
	Reading level is below 7th grade (general) or 10th grade (professional)		
	Every element has text for screen readers to speak		
Purposeful	What the person should or can do to meet their goals is clear		
	The organization's goals are met		
Concise	Buttons have three or fewer words; text is <50 characters wide, <4 lines long		
	Information presented is relevant at this moment in the experience		
Conversational	The words, phrases, and ideas are familiar to the people using it		
	Directions are presented in useful steps, in a logical order		
Clear	Actions have unambiguous results		
	How-to and policy info is easy to find		
	Error messages help the person move forward or make it clear they can't		
	The same term means the same concept, every time it's used		

VOICE			
CRITERIA		**COMMENTS**	**SCORE (0–10)**
Concepts			
Vocabulary			
Verbosity			
Syntax			
Punctuation			
Capitalization			

To provide an example of using the scorecard, let's examine 'appee's onboarding messages. This is the experience that 'appee provides to help people get started when they first sign up. The messages are displayed the first time someone comes to the main screen.

To score the experience, it's helpful to take images or a video of it so that we don't need to set up the experience to remember its details. The important thing is to evaluate the UX text in the context in which people will commonly encounter it.

The three screens of the 'appee onboarding flow start with a message in the center of the screen, over the center of the last challenge-winning image (Figure 6-1). On the second screen, a message points out the bookmark icon in the lower-right corner of that image. The third and final screen has a message that points out the "play!" button at the bottom of the screen.

First message in center of screen, over the center (winning) image

Second message points out bookmark icon to save image

Third and final message points out "play!" button

FIGURE 6-1

The three screens of the 'appee onboarding flow.

To start the scorecard, we need to know what the person is likely trying to do—what is their purpose? And at the same time, what does the organization hope to get out of the experience? Just like for the conversational design exercise in Chapter 3, we begin by listing the goals for the task. For the 'appee onboarding flow, the player's goals are pretty ambiguous: all we know is that they're new to 'appee. The person could be there to upload images, or they could be there to browse images, save them, comment on them, or buy items with images on them.

The 'appee business goals are more straightforward: 'appee wants to reduce the time it takes for a new person to start engaging, to improve the onboarding pace metric. The key behaviors listed at the beginning of this chapter still apply: 'appee wants people to save, comment, and like images, upload images, browse images, and buy items with those images on them.

These goals fill out the first part of the scorecard template (Table 6-2). This is what the UX content is supposed to be doing for the person and for the organization. To keep the scorecard usable for the team, the goals are kept brief and contextual.

TABLE 6-2. The goals for 'appee onboarding, as entered into the UX content scorecard

UX CONTENT SCORECARD FOR: 'APPEE ONBOARDING	
Person's goals	Ambiguous—could be to save or react to images, play a challenge, start their own profile, or buy an item
Organization's goals	Make sure people know what they can do when they're just getting started, especially saving, commenting, and liking, given that those actions inform the machine learning model and help us personalize ads

Now that we have the screens, and we know what the goals are, we can get started scoring the UX content.

ACCESSIBLE

The most essential usability is accessibility. If people can't access the experience, they can't use it! For the purpose of measuring the accessibility of UX content, we have three criteria: language availability, reading level, and labeling.

Available in the languages the people using it are proficient in

Language is the most basic of all access. For example, the US Census records more than 350 languages spoken in the United States, with *8% of the population having limited English proficiency (LEP)* (*https://www. migrationpolicy.org/article/limited-english-proficient-population-united-states*). If an experience is released only in English in the United

States, we could give it a 9.2 on our 10-point scale. This isn't a bad score, but it does acknowledge that the experience isn't usable by 8% of the population based on language alone.

Language might seem like an outlier in the scorecard, because the language the experience is available in isn't limited to the onboarding messages. But localized messages are frequently delivered more slowly than the native language of the experience. When the UX content is newly updated, there can be a delay of a few days to a few weeks before people will be able to use it in other languages.

For 'appee onboarding, the organization has emphasized language accessibility. They have a hypothesis that people will play more if the challenges are in their native language, and their parent corporation operates in several countries. For this criterion, 'appee gets 10 out of 10 points (Table 6-3).

TABLE 6-3. The 'appee onboarding experience gets a perfect score in the language criterion for accessibility in the UX content scorecard

USABILITY	CRITERIA	COMMENTS	SCORE (0–10)
Accessible	Available in the languages the people using it are proficient in	Yes—available in en-US, zh-TW, es-MX, jp-JP, fr-FR, fr-CA[1]	10

Reading level is below seventh grade (general) or tenth grade (professional)

Reading level is another way to measure the accessibility of language. Even fluent speakers of a language might not be fluent readers of that language. Reading for understanding is a skill that requires practice and more attention than most people pay to the labels, titles, buttons, and descriptions inside an experience. Also, there are differences in cognition across the population that affect a person's ability to read— for example, attention deficit disorders, dyslexia, and concussions. Alcohol- and drug-induced impairment matter, too, if you're making an experience that you want people to be able to use while impaired.

---

1   International standard codes for locales (*ISO 3166; https://www.iso.org/obp/ui/#search*) and languages (*ISO 639; https://www.loc.gov/standards/iso639-2/php/English_list.php*) help us to specify which versions of language the experience is available in.

There are several measures available for reading level in English, including the Flesch–Kincaid Grade Level, Gunning fog index, SMOG index, Automated Readability Index, and the Coleman-Liau index. These use sentence length and word length to approximate the minimum grade level in the US school system of a person who would understand the text. *None of these measures are academically validated to use for UX content.* I am eager for colleagues to take on that research and inform us all of the results!

Several free calculators exist online and within several big corporations. To use these calculators, I add periods to the end of any stand-alone phrases, buttons, and labels that don't have them, and then I paste the modified UX content into the calculators. Sometimes, one of the measures provides very different results than the others, but they are often in agreement within half a grade level.

To maximize reading-level accessibility, I keep the reading level below seventh grade for general audiences, and below tenth grade for professional audiences. For our 'appee example, the reading level for any of the tests is at the second- or third-grade level, well under this limit. For this criterion, the onboarding messages get a 10 (Table 6-4).

TABLE 6-4. The 'appee onboarding experience is scored on the reading level criterion for accessibility in the UX Content scorecard

USABILITY	CRITERIA	COMMENTS	SCORE (0–10)
Accessible	Reading level is below 7th grade (general) or 10th grade (professional)	Tests to grade level 2 or 3	10

Every element has text for screen readers to speak

Our final accessibility score is about labeling: every element on the screen should have UX text for the screen reader to speak. This means that any icon, input field, link, or image necessary for understanding should have text that is visible, can be made visible (for example, with hover or mouseover function), or can be made audible (for example, with a screen reader).

The alternate text, whether because of its visible location or auditory information, should be usable to distinguish different actions from one another. In our 'appee onboarding example, the bookmark function is visible in the corner of each image on the main screen. But when the experience was tested, the screen reader said "Button: Bookmark" 10 times! It's not possible for a person to distinguish which one it means, and the experience is reading all the buttons even though they aren't all visible on the screen. This is a bug—a problem that needs to be raised with the engineering team—and it affects the score for this criterion in the UX content scorecard (Table 6-5).

Another impact to this criterion is that the action to take isn't clear. It's not clear if the person is being asked to practice taking the action they suggest, or if the person should tap the message to dismiss it, or if they should tap outside the message to continue. Any of those actions would be common, but the experience needs to specify which it is.

TABLE 6-5. The 'appee onboarding experience is scored on the screen reader criterion for accessibility in the UX content scorecard

USABILITY	CRITERIA	COMMENTS	SCORE (0–10)
Accessible	Every element has text for screen readers to speak	The onboarding message is read, but can't tell what I'm supposed to do with it. Tap it? Bookmarks just read out "Button: Bookmark" 10 times. Can't tell which one is being read, and it's being read all down the screen, even for the ones that aren't visible. Play, Menu, and Profile work.	2

There are more extensive accessibility requirements that don't involve the UX content. Those aren't included in this UX content scorecard because they aren't just about the text, but include the interaction, visual design, and underlying code. It isn't that those things aren't important, but they aren't the theme of this book. Next, let's decide how well the UX content meets the purpose for this experience.

PURPOSEFUL

Being usable includes meeting the purposes that the organization and the people using 'appee have for this part of the experience. These purposes are recorded in the Goals section at the top of the document, but that's not enough. We also need to judge whether the text, as written, will help the person and the organization meet those goals.

What the person should or can do to meet their goals is clear

When they read or hear the UX text, it should be clear what the person should or can do to meet their goal. Like we recorded in the last accessibility criterion, the message doesn't make it clear where or whether the person should tap somewhere on the screen. Without additional indicators (which could be visual design or UX text), the person doesn't know how to meet their purpose. In Table 6-6, the comments record the confusion, and it's given a disappointing score of 6/10.

TABLE 6-6. The 'appee onboarding experience is scored on the person's goals criterion in the purposeful section of the UX content scorecard

USABILITY	CRITERIA	COMMENTS	SCORE (0–10)
Purposeful	What the person should or can do to meet their goals is clear	Not clear whether the bubble is tappable, or whether the person should tap the thing being pointed out. Clear that 'appee wants the person to do something, but not sure how to move forward.	6

The organization's goals are met

The 'appee onboarding experience does a better job of meeting its business purpose than it met the purpose for the person using it. It points out two of the three specific actions listed in the goals, saving and commenting, but liking is left out.

The text also includes buying, which isn't listed in the goals for this experience. The buying is also out of place because a new player probably wouldn't understand what they would be buying. In Table 6-7, the scorer's comments record both where the text is aligned to the organization's goals, and where it isn't.

TABLE 6-7. The 'appee onboarding experience is scored on the organization's goals criterion in the purposeful section of the UX content scorecard

USABILITY	CRITERIA	COMMENTS	SCORE (0–10)
Purposeful	The organization's goals are met	The app points out to tap images to leave comments and buy, but not what they'll be buying; bookmarks cover saving, not liking.	8

In UX content, it's not only important that the text is accessible and meets the purpose. There is limited space and attention for the words, and nobody came to the experience to read the UX text. To be usable, the text must also be concise.

CONCISE

There are two ways to measure concision in the UX content scorecard: the visible length of the text, and whether the text includes ideas that aren't relevant to the person reading it.

Buttons have three or fewer words; text is less than 50 characters wide, less than four lines long

Whether the text is on a large screen (like a television) or small (mobile phone), brief messages are easier to scan. The text that has tested well, in my experience and in proprietary research that I've consumed, has been three or fewer lines long and no more than 50 characters wide. In the same vein, buttons that are one or two words are used more often and faster than buttons with more words. These are challenging limits to meet, but well worth the effort. The 'appee onboarding messages meets all three of these subcriteria as currently written, without even needing a comment (Table 6-8).

Information presented is relevant at this moment in the experience

Limiting the information to just what is relevant to the person may be the most challenging part of writing UX. There are two kinds of problems: first, sometimes we know several different ideas that would be relevant, depending on who the person is. But because we can't always make different experiences for different people, or even know which person is which, we usually need to write one piece of content that every person will encounter. Second, sometimes it's not possible to know what the person would consider relevant. In either case, we just have to do the best that we can.

For the 'appee onboarding experience scorecard, we can note in comments that we can't be sure what the person actually wants, but we also don't know that the ideas we are presenting are relevant to them (Table 6-8).

TABLE 6-8. The 'appee onboarding experience is scored on the two criteria of the concision section of the UX content scorecard

USABILITY	CRITERIA	COMMENTS	SCORE (0–10)
Concise	Buttons have three or fewer words; text is <50 characters wide, less than 4 lines long	✓	10
	Information presented is relevant at this moment in the experience	We're not sure what they want. But because they're new, they should at least be introduced to what's possible. Getting to vote feels out of place. Liking is left out.	8

If an experience were fully meeting its purposes and fully concise and nothing else, it runs the risk of being robotic. That roboticness, by itself, can make the experience more difficult to use. The text in the experience also needs to be conversational.

CONVERSATIONAL

There are many aspects of making an experience feel conversational that have to do with voice, which has its own heuristics. For the parts of conversation that are about usability, it's most important that the experience is using words and concepts that the person would be familiar with, and that those ideas are brought up in a sequence that makes sense.

The words, phrases, and ideas are familiar to the people using it

When an experience uses the words that are most familiar to the person using the experience, the usability of the experience skyrockets. Separate from the terminology (which is in the Clear section, next), the day-to-day words, phrases, and grammar that people would use to describe the experience to their friend or family member are the words that will be most understandable.

In our 'appee example, most of the ideas brought up by the onboarding messages should be familiar to the person if they have used social media or social games in the past. This is an expected background for a person to have before using 'appee for the first time. The one unusual idea is voting: people voting for their favorite challenge image is not a common idea, so a person new to 'appee is not likely to have encountered it before. Bringing it up in the onboarding experience, before that person has the context of uploading images, makes for a weird moment in an otherwise smooth conversation. For this, 'appee loses one point for this criterion (Table 6-9).

TABLE 6-9. The 'appee onboarding experience is scored on the familiarity criteria in the conversational section of the UX content scorecard

USABILITY	CRITERIA	COMMENTS	SCORE (0–10)
Conversational	The words, phrases, and ideas are familiar to the people using it	Voting might not be totally familiar here, as an idea	9

Directions are presented in useful steps, in a logical order

It's important to not only use the words that people easily understand, but to present the ideas to them in the most helpful, logical order possible. People are significantly more successful when ideas are put in the order in which they need to use them. For example, consider the difference between these two statements:

- "To allow location, go to Settings, then turn on Location."

- "To allow location, turn on Location in Settings."

The second sentence is shorter, but puts information in the wrong order. The sequence the person will need to find them is first Settings and then Location.

The 'appee onboarding messages are probably not in the correct order. Even though these directions are not intended to be followed immediately, they neither build on each other nor mimic a person's likely path through the experience. As the comment in the UX content scorecard suggests, it would make more sense to start people with the interactions that are easiest and take the least commitment, before diving into actions that require a higher level of commitment (Table 6-10).

TABLE 6-10. The 'appee onboarding experience is scored on the logical order criterion in the conversational section of the UX content scorecard

USABILITY	CRITERIA	COMMENTS	SCORE (0–10)
Conversational	Directions are presented in useful steps, in a logical order	People are super unlikely to buy as their first action. Nor to leave comments. Order should probably be Save > Like > Comment? Buy might not be the core action...	4

As much usability as is created by creating text that is purposeful, concise, or conversational, it's twice as important for that text to be clear. Without clarity, people can feel good and follow the path but still not have confidence that they understand it.

CLEAR

Paradoxically, clarity is itself a metaphor: it literally means transparent, like clean glass or an unobstructed view. Applying that metaphor to the UX content, it means that the words are doing all that they can to help the person understand the experience. The person has the information they need, and that information makes sense so that they can meet their goal. At the sentence-by-sentence level, clarity is verified by the accessible, purposeful, concise, and conversational criteria. At a holistic level, the UX content needs systems of clarity in place.

The four criteria in the Clear section check for symptoms of systematic clarity. These are attributes that should be present in each part of an experience, from sign-up to the "Sad to see you go" screen. When they are missing in one part, the whole experience suffers. But even though they are systematic criteria, they can apply more or less in each part of the experience. They can also be fixed part by part, message by message, until the whole experience is clear.

Actions have unambiguous results

The actions available to the person using the experience are usually the domain of the interaction designer. But most experiences need to use the UX text on the buttons, titles, controls and more so that the person expects the actions that happen. People should also see or hear when the action is complete. For example, if a person is checking a checkbox, there is a visible change, and a screen reader speaks "checked."

When someone takes a more substantial action, it can be important to give them more robust feedback. For example, when a "Pay Now" button is available in an online purchase, they can reasonably expect that money will be taken from their account. After they use it, the person expects some sort of confirmation that the purchase is complete. If they don't get that set of messages, the person can be left wondering what happened.

Now, imagine that the button at the end of the purchase flow said "Next" or "Continue," and the next thing the person saw was a confirmation that the purchase was complete. The "Next" action had an ambiguous or even misleading result because the person wasn't reasonably expecting to commit to the purchase at that moment.

In the 'appee onboarding messages, people can't determine whether they should tap the message or not. The text inside the messages give a little more clarity to what will happen when the bookmark icon is tapped, but the message makes it seem as if the act of tapping an image will leave a comment or buy it. Even the relatively clear "play!" button becomes less clear, because the message that points to it conflates winning money and voting. Of the 10 points possible, 'appee onboarding messages get only two points (Table 6-11).

TABLE 6-11. The 'appee onboarding experience is scored on the ambiguity criterion in the clear section of the UX content scorecard

USABILITY	CRITERIA	COMMENTS	SCORE (0–10)
Clear	Actions have unambiguous results	Not clear what people should do here, but bookmark text seems clear. PLAY is less clear, because of both winning and voting. Tapping the image sounds like it might leave a comment or buy it?	2

How-to and policy information is easy to find

In any population of people who will use a software experience, there will be people who are comfortable tinkering with the experience until they find what works, and there will be people who don't want to click (or tap) anything until they're sure they will do it right. Most of the people who build software, and those who are in charge of most of the decisions about how an experience is made, are in the first group: we are tinkerers.

Tinkerers like us tend to think that if we're doing our jobs right, people shouldn't need additional help. We take it as a badge of honor when we can set up something new without using the instructions, whether it's an electronic gizmo or an IKEA table. An experience that needs to include how-to information is broken, our thinking goes, because the experience should make it clear what the person should or could do.

But quite a bit of the population aren't tinkerers, according to Margaret Burnett's work on GenderMag *(http://gendermag.org).*[2] Most of the people who could be using software aren't the tinkerers who make software. Most people want to understand the experience before they are comfortable clicking, tapping, or experimenting.

We tinkerers need to get out of our own biases enough to include these people and their money in the experiences we create. To increase usability for all audiences, we can make sure the how-to and policy information is easy to find. When we do this, we not only make more people more capable of using the experience, we also make it more possible for people to enjoy it.

The 'appee onboarding messages are themselves how-to information. There's also help information available in the menu, under Help. On the UX content scorecard, 'appee onboarding messages score 10 out of 10 points for their findable how-to information (Table 6-12).

TABLE 6-12. The 'appee onboarding experience is scored on the availability of help criterion in the clear section of the UX content scorecard

USABILITY	CRITERIA	COMMENTS	SCORE (0–10)
Clear	How-to and policy information is easy to find	This is how-to info; no policy needed right now	10

Independent of the tinkerer/nontinkerer divide, a common place that many people want help is when they reach error conditions. But even better is when the error message is so clear that additional help isn't needed.

Error messages help the person move forward or make it clear that they can't

When a person hits the end or edge of an experience, the experience usually displays an error message. This can be as usable and clear as telling them what to do, or as confounding as describing an underlying technical condition the person has no knowledge of, and no way to affect.

---

2 Mihaela Vorvoreanu, et al., "From Gender Biases to Gender-Inclusive Design: An Empirical Investigation," *Proceedings of the 2019 CHI Conference on Human Factors in Computing Systems* (May 2019), *ftp://ftp.cs.orst.edu/pub/burnett/chi19-GenderMag-findToFix.pdf.*

As described in the Error UX text pattern in Chapter 4, error conditions are among the most important places to empathize with the person reading them. The person is trying to use the experience. They may be there for entertainment or for work, for civic responsibility or as a chore. Whatever they are there for, the error is preventing their progress. The kindest, and most usable, thing the experience can do is to help the person move forward. If they can't be moved forward, the error message should make that clear, so the person can find a different way to meet their own need.

Just like the other criteria, if the 'appee onboarding messages included the possibility of errors, we'd score them as a whole in the UX content scorecard. For example, if there were 10 possible errors, and only 8 met the criteria, the experience would get 8 points. Because the 'appee onboarding messages don't have any error conditions to use as an example, this criterion is marked Not Applicable (N/A), and those points don't count toward the total (Table 6-13).

The same term means the same concept, every time it's used

Our last criterion for clarity is the terminology. Different from other parts of the vocabulary, a term is a word set aside by the experience as having a specific meaning. Terms need special treatment in UX content so that the same idea is always called the same term, and the term isn't used for other actions even when those actions are similar in the experience.

In 'appee, the term for saving an image is "bookmark." Because the onboarding message correctly uses "bookmarks" instead of "saves" (and that's the only term that appears in the messages), the 'appee onboarding messages get points for being consistent about the way it uses the term (Table 6-13).

TABLE 6-13. The 'appee onboarding experience is scored on the last two criteria in the clear section of the UX content scorecard

USABILITY	CRITERIA	COMMENTS	SCORE (0–10)
Clear	Error messages help the person move forward or make it clear that they can't	No error conditions in this flow	N/A
	The same term means the same concept, every time it's used	Bookmark	10

Although we are done with the usability score, there's another important lens to use: Voice. Next, we score the 'appee onboarding messages for voice.

VOICE

Usability is about two-thirds of the possible scores of the UX content scorecard, and voice is the other third. This corresponds well to the goals: the organization and the person using it need the experience to be usable, but the organization is the one that wants to make sure that the voice is recognizable. The person benefits from the recognizable voice, but it isn't their goal.

The criteria for measuring voice come directly from the organization's voice chart (Chapter 2), aligned to the concepts, vocabulary, verbosity, grammar, punctuation, and capitalization it defines.

We defined different aspects of the voice to align with different product principles, so we need to choose which product principles apply to this part of the experience. For example, 'appee has three product principles: Playful, Insightful, and Surprising. The Insightful product principle doesn't apply here, because 'appee relates that only to the images that people upload and comment on. Therefore, the scorecard for the onboarding messages need to include only the voice attributes that apply exclusively to Playful and Surprising in the Criteria column (Table 6-14).

The same way that we did for the Usability section, we can score the 'appee onboarding experience for Voice. Because the Insightful principle was removed, there's no specific guidance for vocabulary, so those points are N/A (Not Applicable). Comments indicate that a few points are lost because sentences were used instead of phrases, a word doesn't need capitalization, and more emojis could be used throughout (Table 6-14).

TABLE 6-14. The Voice section of the UX content scorecard for the 'appee onboarding messages

VOICE	CRITERIA	COMMENTS	SCORE (0-10)
Concepts	Small delights, avoiding grand successes; frippery Unpredictable; misdirection and difficulty can be fun	Lacks small delights, no frippery. There's difficulty, but is it fun?	2
Vocabulary	{Not vocabulary specific}		N/A
Verbosity	Fewer than strictly necessary	These are brief, but they don't leave me guessing in a good way	8
Grammar	Present and future tense Phrases preferred	Could be phrases instead of sentences	8
Punctuation	Avoid periods; use emojis, exclamations, interrobangs, question marks	OK, but why not more emojis?	9
Capitalization	Use capitalization only for emphasis	Inconsistent—does "Tap" need to be capitalized?	9

The most interesting criteria to discuss here are the concepts, a category for which these 'appee onboarding messages get a dismal score. There's no information or small delights included in the messages. There is some difficulty, but the difficulty feels more like usability problems than intentional challenge. Even though from a usability perspective the messages could have been clearer, the concept criteria would make them even more challenging. This is one of many places where, for 'appee, the voice and usability are at odds.

This tension is natural. Throughout human experiences, there are design criteria that contradict one another. Consider them as ends of a spectrum, within which the voice of the experience exists. At different points in the experience, different points on that spectrum of voice are appropriate. Examples are all around us: traffic signs are both highly visible and not distracting. Museums collect and preserve artifacts but also display and use them. Hospital devices can attract the attention of medical staff but let patients sleep.

Games are a special case in which usability is intentionally thwarted. Part of what makes a game fun, whether it's a puzzle or a first-person shooting game, is that there is inherent challenge. That challenge isn't always reflected in the words, but 'appee is constructed to make the words challenging. By scoring the trade-offs between voice and usability scores, a team can record where and how those decisions were made, and choose to make adjustments.

We've now completely scored the 'appee onboarding messages. We can add up the 125 points earned and divide them by the 170 points possible in this task to get the total score of 73% (Table 6-15).

TABLE 6-15. The completed UX content scorecard gives the 'appee onboarding experience a total score of 73%

UX CONTENT SCORECARD FOR: 'APPEE ONBOARDING			
Person's goals	Ambiguous—could be to save or react to images, play a challenge, start their own profile, or buy an item		
Organization's goals	Make sure people know what they can do when they're just getting started, especially saving, commenting, and liking, given that those actions inform the machine learning model and help us to personalize ads		
USABILITY			
CRITERIA		COMMENTS	SCORE (0–10)
Accessible	Available in the languages the people using it are proficient in	Yes—available in en-US, zh-TW, es-MX, jp-JP, fr-FR, fr-CA	10
	Reading level is below 7th grade (general) or 10th grade (professional)	Tests to grade level 2 or 3	10
	Every element has text for screen readers to speak	The onboarding message is read, but can't tell what I'm supposed to do with it. Tap it? Bookmarks just read out "Button: Bookmark" 10 times. Can't tell which one is being read, and it's being read all down the screen, even for the ones that aren't visible. Play, Menu, and Profile work.	2

Purposeful	What the person should or can do to meet their goals is clear	Not clear whether the bubble is tappable, or whether the person should tap the thing being pointed out. Clear that 'appee wants the person to do something, but not sure how to move forward.	6
	The organization's goals are met	It points out to tap images to leave comments and buy, but not what they'll be buying; bookmarks cover saving, not liking.	8
Concise	Buttons have three or fewer words; text is <50 characters wide, less than 4 lines long		10
	Information presented is relevant at this moment in the experience	We're not sure what they want. But because they're new, they should at least be introduced to what's possible. Getting to vote feels out of place. Liking is left out.	8
Conversational	The words, phrases, and ideas are familiar to the people using it	Voting might not be totally familiar here, as an idea	9
	Directions are presented in useful steps, in a logical order	People are super unlikely to buy as their first action. Nor to leave comments. Order should probably be Save > Like > Comment? Buy might not be the core action...	4
Clear	Actions have unambiguous results	Not clear what people should do here, but bookmark text seems clear. PLAY is less clear, because of both winning and voting. Tapping the image sounds like it might leave a comment or buy it?	2
	How-to and policy information is easy to find	This is how-to info; no policy needed right now	10
	Error messages help the person move forward or make it clear that they can't	No error conditions in this flow	N/A
	The same term means the same concept, every time it's used	Bookmark	10

VOICE			
CRITERIA		**COMMENTS**	**SCORE (0–10)**
Concepts	Small delights, avoiding grand successes; frippery. Unpredictable; misdirection and difficulty can be fun	Lacks small delights, no frippery. There's difficulty, but is it fun?	2
Vocabulary	{Not vocabulary specific}		N/A
Verbosity	Fewer than strictly necessary	These are brief, but they don't leave me guessing in a good way	8
Syntax	Present and future tense. Phrases preferred	Could be phrases instead of sentences	8
Punctuation	Avoid periods; use emojis, exclamations, interrobangs, question marks	OK, but why not more emojis?	9
Capitalization	Use capitalization only for emphasis	Inconsistent—does "Tap" need to be capitalized?	9
Total points			125
Points possible			170
Score			**73%**

This raises the question: is 73% a good score? The scorecard is a proxy measurement for how well the UX content meets the goals of the organization and the people who use the experience. The score lets us predict how much we can improve the quality of the text, by putting a value on how closely the UX content comes to being usable and in the voice defined for the experience.

More important than the numeric score, we have performed an analysis that has identified steps that we can take to improve the UX content. Our hypothesis is that we can take these steps to improve UX content quality, which will improve the experience's ability to help the organization and the people meet their goals.

Here are the lowest scores come from these criteria:

Accessible
> Every element has text for screen readers to speak

Conversational
> Directions are presented in useful steps, in a logical order

Clear
> Actions have unambiguous results

Concepts
> Small delights, avoiding grand successes; frippery; unpredictable; misdirection and difficulty can be fun

The team, armed with this information, can decide and prioritize the work to be done to improve the experience. They can score other parts of the experience, like playing a challenge, buying an item, or leaving a comment, and decide which parts need the most investment to achieve a higher score.

Over time, the team can make improvements to the text and score it again. When it compares the difference in the text scores to its improvements in engagement, retention, cost reduction, and other direct measurements, the team can identify how closely this proxy comes to the business outcomes they seek.

Summary: If You Like It, Put a Value on It

Humans can't improve when they don't have feedback. We can make changes, but we can't determine whether those changes are good or bad if we aren't paying attention. This chapter has been all about methods of paying attention.

As we make improvements to the UX content, we should realize improvements in engagement, completion, retention, referrals, and speed to onboarding. These improvements might be small, but they are worthy—and they add up.

We can get closer to understanding why UX content is effective when we conduct research, including interviewing people and analyzing their complaints and questions. People will tell us their feelings, their preferences, their likes and dislikes. They'll tell us how the experience works for them, and they'll usually be as accurate as they can. But just like the people on the team, the people who use the experience can be wrong about why they do what they do, and why they like what they like.

That's why the heuristic measures are valuable, even when the team can use A/B testing and research. The usability heuristics are a set of guidelines that have been generally true about UX content, regardless of an individual person's beliefs about why they behave in certain ways. The voice heuristics are a set of guidelines about what the organization believes is true for them, their experience, and the people who use their experience. Together, the heuristics are a hypothesis of why and how the UX content can be good. When they are applied to an experience, the scorecard gives us a path forward to fixing the words—and help us to understand when it's not the words that need to be fixed.

[7]

Tools of the UX Writing Trade

It's best to have your tools with you. If you don't, you're apt to find something you didn't expect and get discouraged.
—**STEPHEN KING, WRITER**

THERE ISN'T ANY ONE magic tool to be a good UX writer. In fact, most UX writers use widely available tools, even tools that are available for free. In this chapter, I share the tools I use to be successful while I accomplish the main tasks of UX writing:

- Drafting

- Reviewing

- Publishing

- Tracking work

Write for the Context

When most people think of writing, they think of writing words that people will read in a book, article, essay, student paper, or blog. This book has sentences grouped in paragraphs, organized in sections and subsections, to do its word-based work. I used two common word-processing programs, and I wrote it in approximately the same format you're reading it now.

In contrast, UX writing is not a sequence of words, sentences, and paragraphs that stand on their own. Instead, it exists to be the conversation between the experience and the person using it. The experience talks to the person with words and visuals, and the person responds by interacting with elements on the screen.

To choose the appropriate words while UX writing, we need to consider not only titles, sections, and paragraphs, but also buttons, controls, fly-outs, dialogs, text input fields, and more. Our words can be seen, heard, or both. When the person encounters this writing, they don't progress from the top to the bottom of a screen, but rather their eyes flick from top to bottom, from title to button, and might skip all of the words we write.

So, why would we imagine that we could use the same tool to write for an experience that we use to write for a book? If I were to write the UX text in a written-page format, even in tables or a spreadsheet, I would fail to design for the context.

To write for UX, I need to set myself up for success: I need to write the words and evaluate them on the screen where they will appear. Then, I will need to try many options, and save many iterations.

DRAFTING ON SCREENSHOTS

Frequently, the UX writer needs to work on words that have no design file prepared. Maybe that is because the screen was built from a common framework, so developers didn't need pixel-perfect images. Or maybe it was built long ago or by a different team. For any number of reasons, you don't have a design to edit—all you have is a screenshot, attached to a bug, email, or Slack conversation, that says, "This doesn't sound right to me..." For example, Figure 7-1 is an 'appee screenshot with an error message that's incomprehensible to the player.

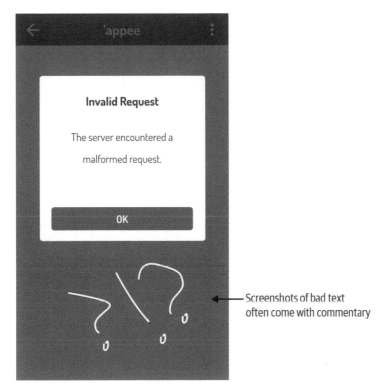

Screenshots of bad text
often come with commentary

FIGURE 7-1

This screenshot of a poor error message in 'appee illustrates a common problem: errors are often written from the perspective of the engineer instead of being designed to be understood by the person using the experience.

Unfortunately, words captured in a screenshot aren't editable: they exist as pixels, not as text that can be typed, deleted, and edited.

To make a version that I can edit, I begin by pulling the image into any of these pieces of software: Sketch, Figma, Microsoft PowerPoint or Google Slides, or even Paint. Any of these will work because they all have these two tools available: text boxes and rectangles.

My goal isn't to make the new text pixel-perfect. I only need the pixels to look good enough that they don't distract from evaluating the new text options that I write. I can do almost the same work using pencil and paper (and do, if I need to!) but the electronic version will be more useful to iterate, share, and convince others.

I create an editable version by drawing a text box over the text that I want to change. It might seem backward, but I begin by typing in the same text that already exists. Then, I adjust the font, size, and style of the text until it matches the original. Sometimes I don't have the correct font installed, so I choose one that is close. Again, my goal isn't perfection, but to get close enough to evaluate.

This text box will be the top layer of a three-layer image. The screenshot itself is the base layer. Now I need the middle layer to block out the existing text, so I draw a rectangle the same size as the original UX text and make it the same color as the background color of the text. I now have three layers: the text on top, then the plain rectangle that blocks out the old text, and then the original image underneath (Figure 7-2).

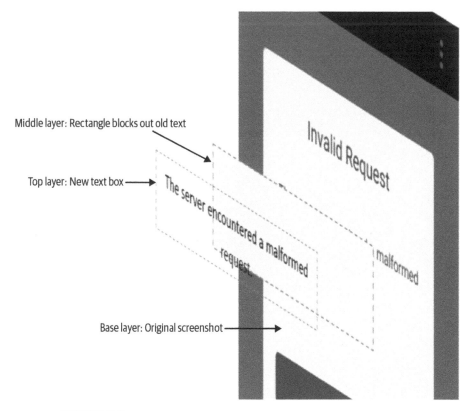

FIGURE 7-2

If we could take a text box and rectangle placed on top of a screenshot and look at it from the side, we would see the three layers stacked one atop the other. The editable text box has the original text in it, which will be my starting place for editing.

To write my drafts, I make a copy of the entire group and then edit the text (Figure 7-3). Then, I make another copy and edit the text again. In general, I'll edit and make copies until I have several good options to choose from.

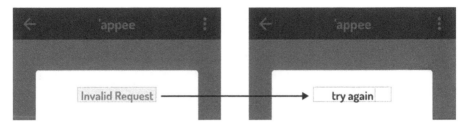

FIGURE 7-3
To start editing, I try out new words in the text boxes I just added to the screenshot.

I continue to iterate new options until I have a few that I think will work (Figure 7-4). For more detail about the editing process, go to Chapter 5.

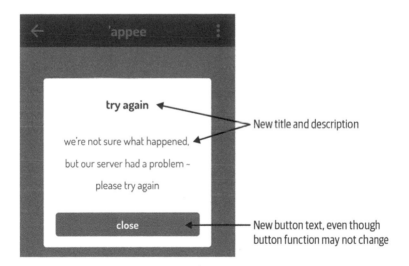

FIGURE 7-4
The result of editing the error message in Figure 7-1 includes changes to every piece of text.

I take the best of the options and share them with the team in a content review document (described in the "Managing Content Review" section, next). Allowing the team to review the UX text in the context of the design makes it possible for them to understand the impact the new words will make.

DRAFTING IN DESIGNS

When I'm working with a designer, whether it's a new experience or updates to an existing one, they usually have a working file in a UX or graphic design tool like Sketch, Figma, or Photoshop. When I work in the same tool, I can iterate the UX text more rapidly and communicate with designers more effectively than any other way.

In an ideal sense, it would be great to know what's being designed while it's being designed. But there are very few tools that make it easy for people to collaborate on designs. The essential ingredient is not the tool, but the commitment a designer and writer can make to collaboration. Some designers and UX writers can pair-design the way some engineers pair-program. But even when they can't or don't work simultaneously, the designs and UX text can be revised by both designer and writer, iterating the text and designs in turn.

In many ways, using a design tool is similar to using text boxes and rectangles to edit screenshots. It doesn't matter whether the text is standing alone or part of a group, symbol, or component. I just need to be able to get to the text box, edit the text in it, and save several versions of the screen as I work. Just like with the screenshot options, I eventually have a set of best options that I can share with the designer and the rest of the team.

Managing Content Review

After the UX content is drafted, it generally needs to be reviewed by a wide range of teammates. This could include the engineers, UX researchers, designers, product managers, attorneys, marketers, and more.

This larger process is not co-creation with the wider team, because the UX writer still has responsibility for the content. But the feedback, ideas, and concerns of each team member should be addressed. It's important to believe that the entire team is trying to make the best possible experience for the people who will use it, and the best outcome for the organization.

The purpose of the review document is to create a bridge between the smaller team that collaborates closely on the design and this larger group of reviewers. It allows team members not only to make suggestions and comments, but also to discuss those suggestions and comments in one place, asynchronously. At the end, there should be a set of UX text and designs that everybody agrees on, with text that can be copied and pasted (instead of retyped) into code.

The single tool that I've found to be easiest and cheapest for the entire team (from legal to engineering to marketing to design, etc.) to use is a text document, like the files produced by Microsoft Word or Google Docs. I am hopeful that more tools for collaboration will become widely available and accepted. But until then, I will share this relatively manual method of storing and sharing documents online so that asynchronous comments can be shared by the entire review team.

In the review document, I include an image of the screen so that people can review the suggested text in place. Beside it, I list the text for the screen in an editable and commentable form. The document has room for any alternate ideas or variations that we're still working out.

For example, Figure 7-5 has the content review document for April Challenges in 'appee. I put the context for the document at the top—in this case, how many challenges are needed and the overall theme for the month. Then, I copy and paste images and text from the design document.

Challenges for April 2019

April summary:

- 30 challenges with 3 emergency backups
- Texture and color: make the most of springtime colors, Easter; note that it's autumn below the equator!

Design	Element	Suggested text
1. current challenge **FUZZY** floofy or feathery, blurry or baffling what makes you feel warm or cozy, or dazed and confused?	Title	FUZZY
	Description	floofy or feathery, blurry or baffling What makes you feel warm or cozy, or dazed and confused?
2. current challenge **fresh as a** breeze, baby, daisy, clean laundry, radish, car wash,	Title	fresh as a
	Description	breeze, baby, daisy, clean laundry, radish, car wash, new guy at work

FIGURE 7-5

April Challenges in a content review document for the 'appee team to review.

When the document is ready, I send it to all of the reviewers. Usually, this is in email or on a group messaging system, where I give the link and the timeline for review. For example, I might write an email to the reviewers:

> Subject: Review April challenges before Noon, March 25
>
> April challenges are ready for your review!
>
> These need to be coded before March 26 to be tested. If I don't hear from you before **12 Noon on March 25**, I'll take that silence as approval.
>
> Please comment in this doc: {link}

When people comment and make suggestions, everyone on the team can see those in the document (Figure 7-6).

FIGURE 7-6

Michelle has already made comments and suggestions in the review document for April Challenges.

When all of the reviews are complete, I work with the designer, developer, or content management system, as appropriate, to publish the final text.

Publishing the Text

To become part of the final experience, UX text must become part of the code. Usually, that means a work-tracking item is assigned to an engineer, with the final designs and text review document linked to that item. The engineer will enter each piece of text and include a comment for each piece of text about its purpose, context, and any special accessibility or localization instructions. The coder will also add error messages as the need becomes apparent, sometimes unbeknownst to the writer, designer, or product owner.

When the code is ready to review, error messages and all, the UX writer receives a code review request. This is our best chance to check for typos before they go into the build as well as to check that the designed text was entered correctly. If there are new error messages, I'll check them and suggest alternative text if necessary. I'll also check that the engineer's code comments reflect the purpose of the content.

A few organizations have created special interfaces for UX writers to publish updates to UX text themselves. In the case of the 'appee challenges, it would make sense for the team to build a way for the challenge text to be updated without having to release new code. I have used content publishing interfaces as simple as text entry fields, and as complex as coding custom XML. If the UX writer is the person entering the text, comments, and notes, asking someone else to check for typos and verify comments is a best practice.

Tracking the Content Work to Be Done

There are very few people on any team who work throughout the software development life cycle the way a UX writer does. There isn't an obvious way to become aware of all of the work to be done, nor to keep track of it, nor to prioritize it.

When there is so much work to be done and that work is distributed across so much of the organization, it can be difficult for the leaders in the organization to understand how much work is getting done. The easiest way to show them is to track the work from the beginning.

I prefer to use a work item, bug, or ticket-tracking system, like Azure DevOps, Jira, Trello, or an internal tool at the organization. As long as the tool will hold the data we need, it will work. It's most useful if the engineering team, design team, support team, and UX content team are all on the same system so that we can pass tasks back and forth to work on them. But if the teams are inconsistent in the systems they use, it's OK to set up one specific to UX content.

The most basic information I need in any given work item is the following:

- Definition of the task

- Priority

- Current status

- Files or links to files

- Date the ticket was created

- Date the last change was made

To provide the simplest example, suppose that I work at 'appee and I find out about new UX content: 'appee will be adding a new direct-message feature for people playing in a challenge. I open a work item to track the UX content work for that feature.

When the product owner has a meeting to kick off the work, I start a new document to take notes. I add a link to that document in the work item. I also add links to the product owner's document. At the end of the meeting, I add pictures of the whiteboard to the same work item.

I also open work items to track work that I initiate as a UX content project, like the rewrite of an existing UX flow. Whatever work is needed, it's a matter of seconds to make a ticket for that work, and I know that I'll keep track of it.

I can assign each work item to the team member who needs to take an action on it, whether it's the legal partner whose approval is needed or the engineer who needs to code the text. When it's assigned to me, I know that I have work to do; when it's assigned to them, they know it's their turn.

When I'm organized, I can feel confident that I'm working on the highest-priority UX content work. The tracking system lets me sort work items by status, priority, person it's assigned to, the date it was created, or any other criteria in the list. I can use the links and content attached to the work items to organize the work and remind myself about what's needed next.

Tracking the work allows a single, reputable answer to the question, "How much work is there?" When business decision makers, department heads, and product leads ask where UX content is most needed, I can sort the work items to let me answer with the number and priority of work items.

Similarly, tracking work items helps me tell the story of the content team's contributions and speak to the impacts that we make. At the end of a project or review period, the accomplishments are easy to summarize by team and priority, to showcase their impact.

Summary: The Tools Are a Means to an End

There are a variety of tools for UX writers to use to create excellent UX content. But mastery of any of these tools isn't the point of UX writing. Using Sketch, Google Docs, or Excel, even at an expert level, won't make you a better writer.

Instead, the UX writer must be willing to use the tools they have to bring empathy and analysis to each interaction a person will have with the words in an experience. We need to draft, edit, and iterate the text using our skill with language to unlock the potential of the experience. We must shepherd stakeholders through a review process to make sure we meet the goals of the organization and of the person.

[8]

A 30/60/90-Day Plan

Nobody plans to fail. They just fail to plan.
—UNKNOWN, ATTRIBUTED TO MANY

IN THIS CHAPTER, I distill and explain the plan I've used in my first 30, 60, and 90 days in three teams, of three sizes (350, 150, and 50 people), at three different companies (Microsoft, OfferUp, and Google). Each time, I joined the team with some idea of the opportunity and a glimmer of the problems I would face, learned from the interview. Each time, the team brought me in because they realized they 1) had a problem with words, and 2) knew that they didn't know how to fix it.

The actual number of days is an estimate, not a rule, but they have been pretty accurate for me. Most usefully, the 30/60/90 structure creates three phases in which ramp-up work can be done thoroughly but quickly—and definitely not perfectly. Their purpose is to fix the words; this method helps me to create a basis for collaboration and iteration that makes the whole experience better.

The First 30 Days, AKA Phase 1: What and Who

The first 30 days is all about learning the experience, the people who will use it, and the team of people who build it. To be successful, you need to know what's important to each of them. At the same time, you need to build the team's confidence that the time, energy, and money they spend on content will pay off.

Your first task is to find a couple of key teammates to gain the widest possible perspective on the organization. Those two or three teammates have a couple of key characteristics: they have broad knowledge of the organization, and they know why the organization decided to "fix the words." In the best-case scenario, they also have different points of view from each other.

You should ask these key teammates the following, in one-on-one, face-to-face meetings: Who is on the team? That is, who will affect what people will encounter in the experience we're making? Write down names from marketing, design, engineering, product owners, program managers, support agents, forum moderators, trainers, attorneys, business analysts, and executives. In the meeting, try to draw a diagram of the organization and ask these key contacts to correct the drawing.

Then, you should request half-hour meetings with each of those 5 to 20 people you've just found out about. There are two purposes for these meetings. First, to gather information about the organization, product, goals, and customers. Second, and just as important, is to introduce people to the idea of working with you. As of this writing, the vast majority of people who make software have never worked with a UX writer, and even fewer have worked with a UX writer who seeks to meet business goals—a UX content strategist. By meeting one-on-one, you get the opportunity to introduce them to what it will be like to work with you, and with somebody in our discipline.

In your invitation, you should write something like, "Hi, I'm the new content person on product X. Your name came up as a person who's important to the product and team, and I'm hoping to learn more from you." Next, choose a time that's likely to be convenient for them, and make sure that you have enough time in your calendar to consolidate learnings between meetings.

To prepare for the meetings, make a mostly empty document, whether that's a slide deck or text document (Figure 8-1). You can use headings to create structure and then fill in the information that you know so far. I recommend keeping the document rough and unpretty to make it clear that you're spending time learning the information, not "polishing" the presentation. It's also shareable, and you'll want to make the link or document available to the people you meet with.

Before the meetings, try to add the information that you think you know, in the briefest, most scannable form. Where you don't know anything yet, leave the slide or section empty. By doing so, you communicate 1) what you want to know, 2) that you know that you don't know it yet, and 3) that sharing these things will be valuable to you. Then, you're prepared to not only take notes in the meetings, but also organize and give context to the information that you're getting.

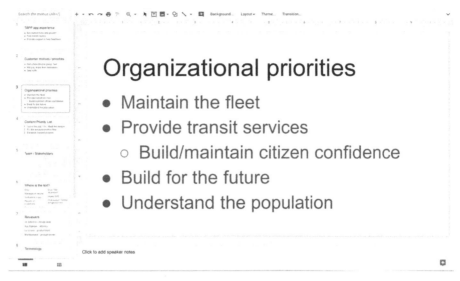

FIGURE 8-1

My content strategy notes have separate sections about the experience, the customer and organizational priorities, the initial content priorities or tasks, a diagram of the team and stakeholders, and places to add info about the channels, platforms, terminology, and reviewers.

This first document contains the following sections:

1. Definition of the experience

2. Customer motives

3. Organizational priorities

4. Priorities for content strategy

5. Team/stakeholders

6. List of existing content

7. Reviewers

8. Terminology

During the meeting, the important thing is to start to build the working relationship with the person you're meeting with. To do that, and also to gain more information, you should discuss the experience, customer, business, and priorities. If the other topics come up, listen, take notes, and move on.

Here are some example questions that I ask:

- What's the most important part of the experience?

- Who are the customers? Is a customer someone who installs, someone who uses, or someone who buys within the experience? If it's an experience people use at work, are the customers the people who buy it or the people who use it?

- How do these people solve the problem right now? How is that experience different?

- What's important to them? What motivates them? What are their priorities, their desires? Do we know what they like or dislike?

- Among the people making and supporting the experience, who will be an ally in making a great experience? What are their motivations, hopes, desires for it?

- In the organization or industry, is there anything working against us? Is there anything working in our favor?

- What's the most important thing I can work on?

- Where are the words broken, or where can the words help the most?

As you listen and learn, you present the document and take notes at the same time, as much as possible. That way, you can show in real time that you're adding that person's priorities to your priority list, and adding their information to your understanding. If what they say is already represented, ask them to check and correct what's there.

Between meetings, consolidate what you've learned. Note taking can become very messy! Sometimes I add notes directly to my document, and sometimes in comments. Sometimes, we use a whiteboard or paper, so I take pictures of those to consolidate later.

Some of the most valuable knowledge that comes out of these meetings is the list of existing content. In my experience, if a team has been working without a content professional, nobody actually knows what all of the content is. No single person has a coherent view of all the content that a person using the experience might encounter.

So, when somebody mentions a folder, repository, content management system, or other source of UX content (for example, UX text, help content, social media engagement, emails, notifications, websites, or canned responses), I add it to my notes. Any content that affects the person's experience is part of the content story. It's content I should be aware of, even if I never work on it.

Similarly, my ears perk up whenever I hear words used with special or unusual meanings. I add those to my notes as a nascent terminology list. As I build the list of terms, I attempt definitions of those terms. When those terms come up, I ask teammates to check and correct my understanding. By using a common, sharable tool to create clarity for myself, I also help the team create a common understanding of the terminology we use.

As your understanding of the experience begins to mature, try to draw the life cycle of the experience. You can begin with the cycle in Figure 1-9, and adjust it for the experience you're working on with this team. You should show the journey of a person through the cycle of investigating, verifying, and committing to trying the experience, then setting it up, using it, and hopefully coming to prefer it. Then, you can adjust the length of sections to reflect the reality of this experience, this organization, and the people who will buy and/or use this experience, at this moment in time (Figure 8-2).

When you have the experience drawn, add it to your notes. As your meetings continue, you can use the diagram to ask members of the team where they think the experience isn't working. You also can use it to explain what you're there to do: you will be making the content that will help spin the wheel, for the organization and for the people who will use the experiences you make.

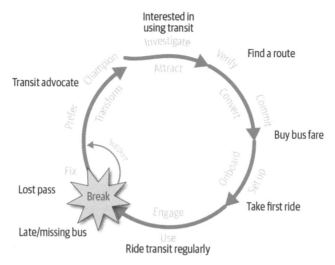

FIGURE 8-2

A diagram of the virtuous cycle adjusted to show the TAPP experience. TAPP attracts people when they are interested in using transit, converts them by providing routes and fares that will work for them, and onboards them by selling them fares and passes. They start to use TAPP with their first ride and might engage to the level of using transit regularly. A person could become so enthusiastic about their experience with TAPP that they become an advocate for using transit, and bring other people into using TAPP.

By the end of the second week, if not earlier, you might begin to receive tactical requests to fix the words: "Can you rewrite this email? What should go in this error message?" I start these first writing tasks in parallel to my learning about the organization and the experience, because the strategy will work only if the writing can get into the experience.

These first writing tasks are a great testing ground for the ideas percolating in your brain about who the people are that will use this experience, what your organizational purpose is, and how the person's and organization's priorities could be expressed in the UX.

This is also an opportunity to demonstrate how you work: asking questions about goals and purposes, measurement of success, and drafting UX text in the designs. This might be your first time working in a designer's file or with a copy of that file. More likely, you have a screenshot of bad text on a screen, which you will edit to provide different text (Chapter 5). The person requesting the text might expect nothing more than an email or chat message with the new words to use, but you have an opportunity to demonstrate that UX text should always be reviewed as part of the design, the way the person will encounter it.

Before you write, search for existing resources about voice or tone, if they aren't already in your notes. These could be brand guidelines, voice charts, style guides, or principles, or they might not exist at all.

You can use what you know so far to write at least three good options for the content. Make them as effective as you can to meet the purpose the person will have for that UX text, and the purpose the organization has for that screen. Strive to make the options as different from one another as possible. Those three options let the team have a good conversation about the purpose for the UX text and to build their understanding about the power of what you can do with words.

To the person who requested the text, you need to explain the reasons why any one of the three options might be the right choice. Often, I learn more about the problem at this time, and I need to draft more options! This revising is a normal part of the process, and it lets me understand the experience and the organization at a practical, hands-on level.

When you agree on one or more of the text options, ask the following: "Who else should be reviewing this?" You might suggest some names that you learned from your interviews, and use the names they recommend. Next, send your first requests for review, listing your recommendation first, and one or two alternates, including the reasoning.

At the end of these first 30 days, you will have talked to most of the right people, you'll be in most of the right meetings and internal communication channels like group emails and chat groups, and you'll have drafted your first text.

At this stage, the document that you started at the beginning of the month now contains at least the following:

1. A prioritized list of tasks to produce or improve UX content

2. The motivations and priorities of the people who use the experience

3. The organization's priorities and constraints

4. Beginnings of lists: channels, terminology, content reviewers

5. Links or images of first, tactical content work

You're ready for Phase 2 when you have built new relationships with your team and have equipped yourself with the information contained in your notes.

30–60 Days, AKA Phase 2: Fires and Foundations

In this second phase of work, half of your time is spent chipping away at urgent, "on fire" work. Doing the "on fire" work helps provide a content development platform to test, practice, and create the foundational pieces that will help the work go better and faster in the future. It will help you to build your understanding of the team, the experience, and the people who will use the experience. Just as important, it helps build trust with the team: if they say it's broken, they'll see you assessing the problem.

As much as possible during this second phase, you should delay effort on larger, systemic changes. The UX text that you write in this second month is unlikely to be the best writing you'll do for the experience. It won't be consistent, because there's no consistency defined. It won't be in the ideal voice, because voice isn't defined. To do good work on systemic changes, the work must be strategically aligned and prioritized with the development schedule to avoid randomizing the team and fracturing your own attention.

Right now, before those systemic changes begin, is the time to measure the baseline of how the UX content is meeting the goals of the organization and the people who use the experience. It's time to examine the "broken walls" in the experience. If the team can't tell where in the experience people drop out, or where they fail to engage, or where they make the decision to buy or commit, now is the moment to specify and advocate for the measurements, research, or instrumentation necessary to notice a change.

You also should try to use the experience yourself, recording the experience and taking screenshots as you go. If possible, you should consume the usability research already conducted, if it exists. Then, apply heuristic measures to the existing content.

You now need to make an initial report on what you find, including what you know about the behavior and sentiment of people using the experience, and a scorecard of content usability based on the heuristics. These initial reports indicate what's working, what isn't working well yet, and which work you recommend prioritizing.

At first, you can share the report informally with members of the team most directly involved with creating the experience. It's a report that outlines problems in what they already built, so you don't want to share it too widely or with too much fanfare. Everybody who built the experience before you arrived was doing their best and working hard, and you need to respect that. Later, after the experience is improved, you can use the report as a baseline from which to measure improvement.

Myself, while I work on individual content requests and measurement (the "fires"), I also spend time setting up the foundational pieces so that I can work and collaborate faster and more effectively. I set up tools for content creation, sharing, and organization; code environments; partnerships and processes that integrate with the team; and to track, manage, and prioritize the work to be done.

TRACK THE PIECES AND THE WHOLE

You should end the first 30 days with a basic sketch of content work to be done, and work requests will begin to flood in. Some requests are for single pieces of UX text, and other requests encompass hundreds: text through an entire experience, error messages, articles and videos, notifications, and more.

On any given day, you might create and review content with designers, researchers, executives, support agents, attorneys, and in code, on multiple projects. You need to learn how this team uses a tracking system (see Chapter 7, "Tracking the Content Work to Be Done" on page 146) or set up a tracking system to serve as a central place to gather, prioritize, and organize information for UX content tasks. By using a tracking system, you keep yourself and your team (when there is a team) afloat on the flood of work to be done.

When all of the UX content work is tracked, you can understand the scope and shape of the UX content needs at a glance. You can see where most of the work is concentrated, and find out which parts of the organization you haven't engaged enough with, and which parts of the experience you haven't examined. Finding these blind spots in the second month can avoid problems in the future!

MINIMUM VIABLE PROCESS

Knowing the work to be done gives you the scope of the battle, but it doesn't help you fight it. In these second 30 days, you need to have tool-chain conversations with engineering, design, and product teams to learn the process for UX text publishing and code review. The first few projects from the first 30 days can help set the context: did that delivery method work for them? Do they have any feedback? What's the best way to get that person's input?

You'll need to listen to what people expect and need from you, and what tools they expect you to use together. You need to steer the work toward a repeatable process so that not only is your work easier, but all of your stakeholders know what they can expect from you as well. You should advocate for collaboration tools, seeking the simplest possible process.

Solicit feedback from product owners, marketing, and business leaders about the process. You'll want to ask where it should change to best fit with their system. You should help them understand when and how to involve you, and when and how you'll involve them. Try to find out how you should assign work items to engineers and how to use their code review system.

In every team so far, a decision maker in the organization will respond to the new UX content focus by saying, "I want to review every piece of text." In my experience, they have thoroughly meant it, and they also don't want to sit down and walk through the code every time there is a change.

What they have wanted is confidence that the text won't increase the organization's liability. They want to be sure that the text accurately reflects the organization's brand. They want to have the gut feeling that the words "feel right" in the experience. You want to involve this person in the UX content process right away so that they can resume doing their own job without also trying to do yours. It's helpful to draw a basic content process for them (Figure 8-3) and suggest the moments in that process where you will proactively consult them. It gives you something to point to and say, "Right here, let's look at it together. You give me feedback, and I'll make it right."

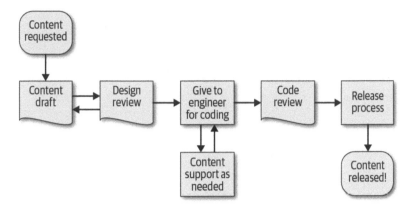

FIGURE 8-3

A basic process for UX content from request, through drafting, review, coding, code review, and release.

DOCUMENT THE CONTENT STRATEGY

To do great work, you need to think systematically about the deep connective tissue of the content: the core terminology and the voice that permeates the conversations the experience has with the people who use it.

Not only do you need these fundamentals of content design, you also need your teams to understand the systemic importance of content. Documenting the content strategy helps you to demonstrate how it is useful to the organization. Creating that documentation takes its own time and energy, but it pays dividends later.

The purpose of documenting any internal strategy is to make future tactical decisions easier, faster, and more consistently. Here are the decisions I use the content strategy for:

- Voice charts guide the direction of content creation and iterations and break ties between good text options.

- Terminology lists create consistency and reduce time spent rehashing choices about how a particular concept is represented in the experience.

- The list of UX content reviewers includes and excludes the appropriate people in the content process strategically, instead of creating tactical political complications.

- Documented priorities and goals focus the content by defining the core UX problems that it helps to solve.

These are living documents, growing out of the notes that you began in the first 30 days, and they need to be further developed. You should review them on a regular cadence (at least annually) and update them when there are organizational changes.

How will you know when you're at the end of the second phase?

You should have passed at least these milestones:

- New content created
- Tracking system and process established
- Poorly performing content updated
- Legal sign-off on a piece of liability-sensitive text
- Marketing sign-off on a piece of brand-sensitive text

At least these indicators of trust have appeared:

- Leaders including me as the responsible party for UX text
- Casual requests to work on individual pieces of text
- Active inclusion in early design thinking

About 75% of this strategic work is complete:

- A tracking system for content tasks
- Alignment about motivations and priorities
- Knowledge of the existing content, and how to access it
- Terminology list
- Voice chart

Another indicator for me that I'm at the end of Phase 2 is a feeling that I'm finally set up to accomplish more. Now, the most urgent, distracting, tactical work is complete and the important foundations are laid. The UX content is ready to have an enormous impact on the quality and effectiveness of the experience. It is time for Phase 3.

60–90 Days, AKA Phase 3: Rapid Growth

The strategy is nearly done, which is as good as a strategy ever gets. It is time to present the strategy as a whole for the first time. The desired outcome of the presentation is to cement the solid foundation: your team and your leaders can have confidence that the content strategy is created considerately, together, and that the work has a purpose. By signing off on the strategy, they validate and support the work to be done.

Communication about the work is a critical part of the work, and might be the most difficult part to accomplish. The presentation includes all of the parts created to date: the tracking process and list of current tasks, the content landscape, alignment on motivations and priorities, terminology list, and voice chart. This summary of the UX content strategy is solid enough that the important (or controversial) ideas are covered, but unpolished enough to indicate that time hasn't been wasted polishing internal documents.

Ideally, everybody at the presentation has participated in the process of creating the strategy. They get to enjoy the fruition of their own work and advice and, accordingly, the results of their decision to hire me.

At this point, you should seek feedback during and after the presentation, because it provides the corrections necessary now to be successful later. If the feedback is that the strategy is wrong, you should thank them for their perspective. If they're wrong, it might be simply that the presentation of the work didn't scratch their itch. If they're right, it's fantastic that you've gotten correction so early. It's only the second (or third) month on the job, so it's the best time to make adjustments. Even the presence of feedback is a good sign, because it means people are invested.

Starting in this third month, you need to set the sustainable pace of how you'll engage in the tracked, prioritized work of UX writing. You should respond to requests and make requests for content changes. You should partner with the team to design new experiences, advocate for the people who use the experience every time they consider the words, and apply and sometimes revisit and tweak the strategy.

Phase 3 is over when the process of creating content for the experience is healthy enough that you can begin to broaden the scope of what content strategy can do for the organization. Now is the time to check in on trends in the field and on the rest of the content being created about the experience. You'll want to work to strengthen connections to be made with marketing, operations, and knowledge management. You should investigate opportunities in the industry, like content-bots using machine learning to prewrite content, and seek out new research, like best practices about titles, labels, accessibility, and inclusion. Some words might still need "fixing," but new UX content will be created strategically, the first time.

Summary: To Fix the Words, Build Strong Foundations

To create UX content that is effective in meeting the organization's goals and the goals of the people who will use it, I start by understanding those goals, my teammates in this adventure, what work they have done, and which work they don't know to do yet. In Phase 2, I fix urgent problems while building the foundations that will help me organize and demonstrate the effect of future work. Phase 3 is the beginning of work that uses the power of content tools from the beginning, to be more effective than ever before.

There are a lot of content accomplishments in this 30/60/90-day plan, but the work that pays the most dividends comes from doing the work visibly, in partnership with the team. By making the content strategy visible in presentations of voice and terminology, the team and executives understand that we've unlocked a new power tool. By making the content tasks visible, the team understands the work it takes for the UX content to advance the goals of engineering, design, and the organization, while it supports the person who will use it. In the process of doing the work, the UX content goes from being a source of pain to being valued.

[9]

What to Do First

A good plan, violently executed now, is better than a perfect plan next week.

—UNITED STATES ARMY GENERAL GEORGE S. PATTON

IF YOU TAKE NOTHING else away from reading this book, I hope you know that the purpose of UX content is to meet two categories of goals: those of the organization and those of the people who use the experience. To meet those goals, you'll need to listen to people, prioritize the work, and collaborate with your team.

Decide What Is Urgent and What Is Important

Prioritizing the work is its own challenge, even when the priorities of the organization and the people using the experience are clear. Even when writing the work is tracked and the process is established, it can be difficult to make sense of what you should do first, or even next.

I like using the *Eisenhower Matrix* for UX content tasks, which categorizes work according to importance and urgency (Table 9-1). Any task or work item is either urgent or not urgent, and either important or not important. The four categories come with implied actions:

- Urgent and important work should be done first.

- Important but not urgent work should be scheduled for later.

- Urgent but not important work should be delegated to people who find it important.

- Work that is neither urgent nor important should be discarded.

TABLE 9-1. The Eisenhower Matrix, as applied to UX content tasks to be done

	URGENT	NOT URGENT
IMPORTANT	**Do** Design new experiences Unblock design, engineering, research Write text that affects liability	**Schedule** Repairing existing, broken text Research into effectiveness and usability Updates to voice and terminology Partnering about design strategy
NOT IMPORTANT	**Delegate** First drafts of common, edge-case, or error text	**Discard** Arguing about grammar, like prepositions at the end of sentences

Work that is both urgent and important should be prioritized over any other work. This includes work that other people are currently engaged in, like developers coding new experiences or updating current experiences, or having just uncovered a failure case for which they need a new error message. This also includes future-facing design and research, keeping designers and researchers unblocked. Designers should have the best possible words before their designs are reviewed, and long before coding. Researchers should have the best possible words in their usability and concept studies to evoke the information that will be the most useful later on.

When work is important but not urgent, we can track it in the work-tracking system and schedule time to do it. This work includes all of the content that UX writers recognize as broken but nobody else is working on. We can make time to create new content for those experiences and lead those projects. These changes are not to be made lightly; we will need to communicate the changes we want and the impact we expect those changes to make. Part of the work will be to articulate how the content underperforms now, and how we will measure the effect of the changes.

When work is urgent but not important, it is not expected to help reach the goals of the people using the experience or the goals of the organization. Writing this text should be delegated to the team member it is most important to. This might be the first draft of a rush-out-the-door experience, notification, or message. Letting other people do the initial UX writing might seem strange, but it's a great way for teammates to express what they need out of the content. They can put far too many words in, and, if necessary, we can glean what they intend, clarify with them, and help them simplify it. It can save time for both of us and give us the opportunity to build a more solid partnership.

When work is neither important nor urgent, it's OK to not do it at all. This includes almost every argument I've had over grammar, commas, and hyphenation, except where the text change would change the meaning of the phrase. Arguments are an important part of the mix of communication in a healthy team, as long as people are basing their arguments on how best to meet the goals of the organization and the people who will use the experience. But even more important is to build the kind of collaboration in which the person responsible for the words can be trusted to make this kind of decision.

Ground the Content in Empathy

When we create experiences, we need to care about the people who will use the experience. When we don't care, we risk failing at our core task: to make experiences that meet our goals.

The root of caring is to believe people about the experiences they have. Their experiences can be similar to your own, or they might be literally unimaginable, but we don't need to imagine them. We must listen to what actual human beings say and observe how they behave and believe that we are hearing their story.

When humans listen to a person's story, they tend to produce the chemical of caring: oxytocin. When writers listen to a person's story, we get that oxytocin and more.

For a writer, the simple act of listening uncovers a gold mine. When people tell their stories, they are likely to use the words they will find recognizable. By listening, the writer learns the grammars that the people already understand. The writer learns the emotional lading of the jargon specific to the people's experience.

When the writer then uses these words, they can create an experience that connects people to the experience without feeling like they are reading.

To write effective UX, work toward understanding the concerns, needs, and the words of the people who will use the experience. Go out and listen to them. Bring them in and listen to them. Watch videos of interviews with them, and seek to understand their point of view. This research will give us an appreciation not only of where they're coming from, but also of how different our own perspective is.

And while we talk to people outside the organization, don't forget the people on the team. These people, with their opinions, viewpoints, perspectives, and prior knowledge, will have an enormous impact on the experience, too. There are people invested in making a great experience all over the organization, including the marketing directors, general managers, directors of design, heads of engineering, engineers coding the feature, program managers, product owners, designers, and the sales and support agents.

Anybody, and everybody, can have opinions about words. How to use those words might not be well understood, especially when there hasn't been a dedicated UX writer.

Introducing UX Content to the Team

If you accept a job as the first content person in an organization, they might think that you're there to "choose the right word" or to "check the words." They probably think of it as a word problem: "We need to explain," or "We need them to understand..." Or, maybe it's a UX problem: "We need words to go on the buttons" or "there are too many words on the screen."

"We need words" is not the problem that we solve as UX writers. We communicate. We invite action. We inspire loyalty. Our teams need to know that UX writing can be used to solve problems. It's up to us to frame our work to reflect the problems we're helping to solve.

I've found it helpful to explain UX writing in terms of programming. Software engineers write in one or more software languages. There are specific grammars and techniques to use in each language to get the best results from the hardware, firmware, and the services on which the software will depend. Those languages are compiled into programs to push the right electrons, at the right moments, to the screens and speakers that people will use.

UX writers write in one or more natural languages. There are specific grammars and techniques to use in each language to obtain the best results from the people and their context. Those languages are compiled by each human as they connect with those screens or speakers to transform those sights and sounds into the right synapses, firing at the right moments, to create a useful, entertaining, or necessary part of their lives.

Therefore, both software engineers and UX writers use the grammars and commands specific to their languages to meet the goals of the organization and the people who use the experience. Both groups work in a process of design, writing, cycles of review and testing, and publishing. Both groups need to be flexible to adjust to idiosyncrasies in the languages, the compilers, the architectures, and contexts the experience lives in. If our teams can work with software engineers, our teams can work with UX writers.

Summary: Use UX Content to Meet Your Goals

Organizations that make experiences are learning the effect that UX content can have when it is written strategically. UX writers, people dedicated to creating UX content, can bring knowledge of best practices, UX text patterns, structures for voice, iterative editing, and review.

Perhaps you are a UX writer, you support a UX writer, or you're considering adding a UX writer to your team. I'm so excited about the future we have in front of us. We have solid work to build upon, and we have so many possibilities ahead as we continue to invent and research best practices. Together, we have the opportunity to help people and organizations meet their goals by creating, iterating, and measuring the UX content.

[*Index*]

About the Author

Torrey Podmajersky helps teams solve business and customer problems using UX content. She has written inclusive and accessible consumer and professional experiences for Google, OfferUp, Xbox, Microsoft account, Windows apps, privacy, and Microsoft education. Torrey's high-intensity speaking style was refined in the crucible of teaching chemistry, but even her most engaging lectures no longer require eye protection. She blogs on Medium and shares ideas on LinkedIn. She co-created the UX Writing Fundamentals curriculum for Seattle's School of Visual Concepts, and has been teaching there since 2016. Torrey has a bachelor's degree in Physics from the University of Washington and a master's in Curriculum & Instruction from Seattle University. She has done freelance fiction writing, home health care work, foster parenting, high-power rocketry, marketing communications, designed the Pilda Pill Sorter, and taught high school science for nine years. Torrey's range of experience helps her empathize with a broad range of people, and she brings that empathy to her products and her teams.

Colophon

The animal on the cover of *Strategic Writing for UX* is a gray catbird (*Dumetella carolinensis*). This group of birds has a wailing call that resembles the meow of a cat, giving them their common name. They are found in North and Central America, favoring a habitat of scrubland and the outskirts of forests.

The gray catbird has mostly gray plumage, with rust-colored coverts under its tail. Though the coloring of this species is nondescript, they have vivid personalities: apart from the cat-like noise, they have a variety of calls (including imitations of other birds) and quirky physical motions like drooping the wings, angling the head, and fanning out the tail. Male catbirds often "riff" for over 10 minutes, at a rate of 90 syllables per minute.

Catbirds have a diet of insects and berries, which they forage for on the ground or within shrubs and trees. Females build cup-shaped nests about 3–10 feet off the ground, and lay 2 or 3 light blue eggs at a time. The catbird is adept at distinguishing its own eggs from those of the brown cowbird (who opportunistically lays eggs in other birds' nests so that the other mother will mistake the cowbird's chicks for her own and raise them). Catbirds will instead eject the incorrect eggs from the nest.

The cover image is a color illustration by Karen Montgomery, based on a black and white engraving from *Brehms Thierleben*. The cover fonts are Gilroy Semibold and Guardian Sans. The text font is Scala; and the heading font is Gotham.

Milton Keynes UK
Ingram Content Group UK Ltd.
UKHW020949180924
448420UK00002B/3